Anglicans and Tradition
and the Ordination of Women

HENRY MCADOO served for twenty-three years in the parochial ministry in town and country, ten of which were spent as Dean of a cathedral until his election as a Bishop in 1962. He was Archbishop of Dublin from 1977 to 1985 and was involved in liturgical revision acting as Chairman of the Holy Communion subcommittee of the Liturgical Advisory Committee which produced the Irish *Alternative Prayer Book* in 1984. Trinity College, Dublin, elected him to an Honorary Fellowship. His published works include *The Structure of Caroline Moral Theology* (1949), *The Spirit of Anglicanism* (1965), *The Unity of Anglicanism: Catholic and Reformed* (1983), *The Eucharistic Theology of Jeremy Taylor Today* (1988), *Anglican Heritage: Theology and Spirituality* (1991; 2nd impression 1997), and, with Kenneth Stevenson, Bishop of Portsmouth, *The Mystery of the Eucharist in the Anglican Tradition* (1995; 2nd impression 1997).

Also by the same author and available from The Canterbury Press:

Anglican Heritage: Theology and Spirituality (1991, reprinted 1997)

The Eucharistic Theology of Jeremy Taylor Today (1988)

First of Its Kind: Jeremy Taylor's Life of Christ: A Study in the Functioning of a Moral Theology (1994)

The Mystery of the Eucharist in the Anglican Tradition (with Kenneth Stevenson) (1995, reprinted 1997)

Anglicans and Tradition
and the Ordination of Women

H. R. McAdoo

CANTERBURY
PRESS
Norwich

First published 1997 by The Canterbury Press Norwich
(a publishing imprint of Hymns Ancient & Modern Limited
a registered charity)
St Mary's Works, St Mary's Plain,
Norwich, Norfolk, NR3 3BH

British Library Cataloguing in Publication Data

A catalogue record for this book is available
from the British Library

ISBN 1–85311–172–4

*Typeset by David Gregson Associates, Beccles, Suffolk
and printed and bound in Great Britain by
St Edmundsbury Press, Bury St Edmunds, Suffolk*

Contents

Foreword

The decision of an increasing number of Provinces of the Anglican Communion to ordain priests who happen to be women has raised a number of important questions that make it impossible to turn the clock back. Repeated criticism from the Vatican, however tactfully expressed, has highlighted the fact that the Anglican way of taking these decisions, and the grounds on which they are made, is different from the Roman Catholic way.

In this important book, Dr McAdoo uses his affinity with the Anglican divines and his experience as Anglican co-Chairman of the first Anglican–Roman Catholic International Commission to demonstrate that to ordain women priests in Anglican churches is in harmony with classical Anglican approaches to the relationship between Scripture, Tradition and Reason. It is not primarily the effect of a passing fad in society or a desire to keep up with the Protestant world – where, it needs to be noted, the issue is not universally agreed. Indeed, one of the major trajectories of this book is the essentially constructive way Anglicans – at their best! – have managed to wrestle with new questions and face the way to solutions, often through conflict. For example, when Richard Hooker or Jeremy Taylor was trying to show that the Church of England was a real church, Catholic and Reformed, they used Anglican formularies to demonstrate the view often held among the early Fathers of the mutual coinherence of the Scriptures and the Church.

But McAdoo does more than simply defend an Anglican position – necessary though this manifestly is, not least when we are in danger of losing our collective memory. He draws attention to the inadequacy of a fundamentalist view of Scripture or Tradition. Each needs the other, and both need Reason – in its imaginative rather than cerebral form – for the Church to respond effectively to new demands. Tradition needs scrutiny; as Paul Avis has observed, 'the place that classical Anglicanism allocates to tradition is favourable though strictly circumscribed'.

There will be those – including some fellow-Anglicans – who will probably remain unconvinced by this extended essay. But the Church Catholic has never been a stranger to controversy and that can be a sign of health. For example, when the Moderator of the General Assembly of the Church of Scotland decided to call on Pope John XXIII – in days when the Roman Catholic contribution to the ecumenical movement was considerably smaller than it is now – a deputation was sent to try to stop him. 'I thank you for your opposition,' came the Moderator's reply. 'It helps to clarify the mind.' And the visit went ahead!

Opinion about the ordination of women is far more subtle and varied than the glib and unfortunate terminology of 'two integrities' can ever encompass. Dr McAdoo's book deserves to be read as an important contribution to the debate, and as an authoritative *apologia* for the Anglican method in self-understanding as well as the development of doctrine.

✝ Kenneth Portsmouth
Advent 1996

Prefatory Note:
On the Reaffirming of
Anglican Identity

This book is in the nature of what our ancestors would have called *A Modest Enquiry* into the Anglican identity in respect of doctrinal authentication and formulation. Within the totality of 'the faith once for all delivered' it attempts an investigation of the working of the Anglican synthesis, the appeal to Scripture, Tradition and Reason, and of the application of this to the question of the priestly ordination of women.

Inevitably it will advert to matters still controversial for some, but it is written in no negative spirit of controversy. Rather does it aim to be a positive statement of Anglican identity. One does not affirm an identity against someone but for someone, looking for that reciprocity which is at the heart of dialogue where the commerce between criticism and value-recognition creates both a comprehension of the other and an unpretentious self-understanding. To underrepresent one's identity is to short-change one's partners in dialogue.

I trust that the book will be regarded in this light and that it may serve to demonstrate convincingly that this identity has been and continues to be historically and consistently affirmed in the life and thought of the Anglican Communion.

H. R. McAdoo

I

The Spirit, Continuity and Change

The use made of the appeal to tradition and the authority accorded to it by some opponents of the priestly ordination of women impel the putting of certain questions. For instance, what is understood by 'tradition'? Is it something given and immutable, a body of thought and practice, or a process of handing these on, or the specific products of the traditionary process? Or is there something of all three in 'tradition' and, if so, which is definitive? What in fact constitutes authentic tradition and what is its force and function in the determining of questions of Christian doctrine and praxis? More immediately, how have Anglicans regarded tradition and in what way have they been accustomed to use it?

Viewed from one angle, these are questions about the *authority* of tradition. They are concerned with its standing in the processes of doctrinal formulation and of ecclesial discipline, with the teaching function of the Church and with the unfolding of the Gospel's implications in historical time and place. From another angle, they are questions about *authentication* and about the *continuity* of doctrine: How do we know that this statement or that practice is authentic Christianity, part of or consistent with 'the faith once for all delivered' – the *hapax* of Jude 3, *tē hapax paradotheisē tois hagiois pistei*? This *hapax* does not mean, as R. P. C. Hanson put it, that revelation is like an inert object dug out of an ancient tomb, but rather that it is *dynamic*. In terms of the content of the Gospel, the *kerygma*, one could say that revelation is closed – 'in these last days he has spoken to us by his Son' (Heb. 1:2) – but that it is a continuing historical

1

dialogue between God and man in which something keeps *happening* as we apprehend revealed truth: 'the apostles apprehended revelation no less than we, but in a different way from those who were later to apply theological reflection to it in the light of later events'.[1] Is there then some determinant which controls the relationship and interaction of continuity and change in Christian faith and practice? And what role does the appeal to tradition fill in this process which is part of the ongoing life of the Church, the community formed by the Holy Spirit and in which He abides: 'for we were all baptised by one Spirit into one body' (1 Cor. 12:13), and 'there is one body and one Spirit ... one Lord, one faith, one baptism' (Eph. 4:4,5)? Are there concepts of tradition which regard it as a (more or less) unwritten *corpus*, a certified accumulation of irreversible precedents, forgetting that 'the mystery of Christ ... is revealed by the Spirit to God's holy apostles and prophets' (Eph. 3:5)?

Can there be any valid concept of tradition which either ignores or qualifies this central reality, the Spirit abiding in the Church? The picture of tradition as delineated by the Orthodox theologian Olivier Clément clearly brings out this element of tradition and is a readjustment needed in much contemporary thinking on the subject: 'Tradition is not a written text with which we can choose to agree or disagree; it is not material suitable for dissection by scholars. It is the expression of the Spirit *juvenescens*, as Irenaeus of Lyons says "in its youthfulness". It is of course our foundation history, but it is also a living force...'.[2] We meet the same theme throughout the handling of his fellow-Orthodox scholar Nicholas Lossky in his outstanding examination of 'the immense patristic and historical learning' of that great Anglican, Lancelot Andrewes – whose devotion, not uncritical, to the Fathers was of the same nature: 'The criterion is, in the last resort, the Truth itself, that is to say Christ, whom the Spirit reveals. Andrewes loves to recall the boldness of the Council of Jerusalem in saying: "It has seemed good to the Holy Spirit and to us" (Acts 15:28).' Lossky further comments that the 'tradition of the Church is not the simple conservation of what has been said or done in the past. It is a *dynamic* process that transcends linear time, without in any way abolishing it. It is, in fact, a way of living in time in the light of eternity, which recapitulates past, present, and future because everything is lived in *contemporaneity with the reality of the Gospel'*.[3] There is much of value for us here and Anglicans have concurred gratefully with the central emphasis on the role of the Spirit, but they are less happy with the Orthodox concept of tradition as being the *totality* of dogma and life in the Spirit. Viewed from one angle, Orthodoxy would appear to regard tradition as covering everything, from the veneration of icons to the Christological dogmas – all are tradition. This removes tradition from the historical time process and puts it outside the range of the critique of reason, as if the Spirit had no part to play in either; and it leaves the questions raised by the Reformation and the Counter-Reformation unasked and unanswered.

We meet both aspects, the stress on the Spirit and the historicity of tradition, in the work of a contemporary Anglican theologian. A. M. Allchin's *The Dynamic of Tradition* (London 1981) traces the riches of tradition in which, to quote T. S. Eliot,

> Time present and time past
> Are both perhaps present in time future.

Allchin takes up the underlying question which we have already noted concerning continuity and change:

> What does it mean to say that we hold the same faith as those who have preceded us by many centuries? ... linked to these larger questions is another set of problems about the way in which tradition functions. If we allow that there is some real continuity of life and thought, *how is it maintained*? Do we remain true to the past by refusing to change, or by being willing to change? How is it that a tradition seems at times able to renew itself from within? ... Can we say that it is the Holy Spirit who is the bearer and creator of the tradition?[4]

The answers which in the course of this book I am attempting to give to Allchin's questions among others involve not only the relationship of continuity and change but the vital matter of criteria for doctrinal authenticity. The bearing of both on what we mean by tradition and how we see its authority and its functioning in the life of the Church is obvious. Central to all is *the Spirit abiding in the Church*, whether we are thinking in terms of the inspiration of Scripture or of the forming of the mind of the Church. Whether we are thinking corporately or individually of our identity as Christians, or of our personal growing to maturity through Word and Sacrament, the Spirit is central to believing, behaving and belonging: 'For we were all baptised by one Spirit into one body.' Then, 'Can we say that it is the Holy Spirit who is the bearer and creator of the tradition', and how does the Church receive, verify and interpret a tradition as being authentic, a gift of the Spirit of truth? This is where criteria and hermeneutics come in, where past and present are in dialogue under the Spirit's guidance in the Church which is a living continuity in a context of change. Richard Hooker, who called the Church 'a body which dieth not', put his finger on this elusive complex of continuity and change when he noted that change, except in fundamental 'articles concerning doctrine', was a reality for the Church which has 'authority to establish that for an order at one time, which at another it may abolish, and in both do well'[5] – and significantly he had been discussing tradition.

The reality, however, for him is the Spirit abiding in the Church who has inspired Scripture and continues to lead and guide the living Church:

> In the nature of reason itself there is no impediment, but that the self same Spirit, which revealeth the things that God hath set down in his law, may also be thought to aid and direct men in finding out by the law of reason what laws are expedient to be made for the guiding of the Church, over and besides them that are in Scripture.[6]

Spirit and change, Scripture and tradition, reason as the Spirit's instrument – all are here, and within and shaping their complex relationship is the eternal Gospel and men's attempts to receive, apply and proclaim it in every age and culture.

> How in the light of a theory of doctrinal evolution should we be able to decide what was an authentic evolutionary change? These questions require us to understand how we believe Spirit and tradition relate. They require of us too a response to questions about the interpretation of Holy Scripture. Is Scripture part of the means by which we identify the Christian community in succeeding ages, and indeed through which we view the evolution of doctrine?[7]

This extract is from a book, *Spirit and Tradition: An Essay on Change* (1996) by Stephen Platten and George Pattison, which appeared after this work had been completed. It sent me back to this point in my own text because it is addressing some of the issues I am investigating, but from a somewhat different angle, that of understanding tradition and the development of doctrine in terms of the model of evolution – though historically it should be remembered that Anglicans have on the whole regarded tradition as dynamic, not static. This evolutionary model is much more convincing than the model put forward by John Henry Newman, that of the unfolding flower: doctrines were there in embryonic form, hidden and gradually developing, 'it had to be this way, pre-determined in apostolic truth'. For Newman, there were obvious ecclesiastical strings attached: 'This meant that the plants now flourishing, the developments now observed and practised in the life of the Church (that is, the Roman Catholic Church), had to be seen as the only possible developments, bearing in mind the nature of the primaeval seeds.' Newman was aware both of the need for continuity and the reality of change, but the question is: Does this theory stand up to criticism when set 'within the wider context of historical consciousness?'[8]

His *Essay on the Development of Christian Doctrine* is striking and original in its attempt to relate continuity and change, but the tension is felt in the conclusion that the developments were inevitable, pre-determined. 'It *had* to be this way.' From the point of view of the authenticating of

→ p. 81, 82 in Sykes (The study of...)

⇒ women's ordination (vergleiche Synode Debate p. 74-76

doctrine, the theory would seem to me to present a practical difficulty, which is this: Does such an approach preclude the conclusion that a given 'development' could in reality be an 'innovation'? Questions have been raised throughout the Church's history concerning 'developments' which are not seen to be reconcilable with or derivable from the *hapax* as set forth in Scripture. One must ask: Is this developmental determinism immune to historical verification and to the discernment of reason? This concern, as we shall see in the course of this study, was voiced by Anglican theologians from Andrewes to Waterland as they raised the problem of doctrinal innovations – for them a major issue.

Platten's and Pattison's own view of tradition is that it is not simply a *means* of communicating, of handing over 'the deposit', but also a *content*, so that 'it is what it is by virtue of what it has to communicate'. The criticism here could be that such an understanding of tradition is shapeless. 'What is it then,' they ask, 'in the process of tradition that ensures such definition? We suggest that it is the fact that tradition comprises a process of active remembering, a process that sustains continuity in the midst of change even as at the same time it generates changes out of that which gives continuity.'[9] The nub here, as I see it, is the problem of content, the problem of seeing tradition as in some sense self-shaping. Is there not the same danger as exemplified in Orthodoxy of calling *everything* tradition? Platten and Pattison are aware of this: 'Yet it remains true that nothing that has been said can justify everything that passes for Church tradition.'[10] Anglicanism has always been alive to this, hence the insistence in formularies and theology alike (the history of which I am here endeavouring to trace), on a deliberate circumscribing of tradition. Tradition is not only the Church remembering but the Church interpreting, so what then ensures authentic interpretation? The answer given is, of course, the Bible – but the Bible and hermeneutics, 'a vital part of contemporary theology ...'[11] In effect, classical Anglicanism, as we shall see, is saying and has always said the same thing: Scripture and reason aided by the

Spirit authenticate the Church's memory and interpretation as it integrates its past with its present situation. It is striking how two contemporary theologians using an original approach with fresh implications for liturgy and for ecumenism prove to be, in essentials, sympathetic to the way in which the theme has been handled in the Anglican tradition from Jewel (Bishop of Salisbury, 1559–71) to Lambeth 1988 and onwards.

I would, however (like Lambeth 1948), lay the emphasis differently and more heavily on the historicity of the revelation to which the Scriptures bear the unique witness. Historicity is the necessary control on dogmatic space-flights. It is because of *this* that tradition has to be controlled by this evidence. It is the fixed centre; and all interpretation and all meditation, all theology and all spirituality, can do no more than circle round it, feeding on it and producing tradition.[12] This is what lies behind the description of tradition which I offer at the beginning of the next chapter. It is the authenticating interplay between the historic revelation, which is a constant, and the process of remembering and interpretation within the living Community of faith which ensures continuity in the midst of change. There is then a sense in which tradition is the living expression of 'the faith once for all delivered' and in the changing context of different centuries and different cultures.

The connection between all this and the priestly ordination of women will, I trust, become clearer as we evaluate the change in the light of Scripture, tradition and reason, for always it is the life-giving Spirit of truth who creates the context as He creates the Community of the baptized.

II

On the Limits of the
Appeal to Tradition

The promise to the Church was that 'the Spirit of truth ...
will guide you into all truth' (John 16:13). Can we then be
far wrong if *we define tradition as the continuing process by
which the living Church through the presence and guidance
of the Spirit interprets and enters into the meaning of the
faith once for all delivered, proclaiming it to each generation
in its own idiom*? But are there then no limits, no deter-
minants in this traditionary process, which will ensure
that what is being 'traditioned', handed on, is authentic, is
original Christianity? 'True Christianity can only be traced
from the real origins', writes Hans Küng, adding, 'only an
awareness of these origins can enable us to determine what is
essential and what is inessential, what is decisive and what is
unimportant, what is permanent and what is transient'.[1] In
other words, there is a determinant, the *hapax*, as my venture
at a definition of tradition suggests, and this gives to
Scripture its primary and controlling role in guaranteeing
both the authority and the continuity of any doctrine. *As we
shall see, this is a feature in the Anglican appeal to tradition.*
Earlier in the same book, *The Church*, Küng has shown how
as a matter of history the question of limits to tradition or
their absence impinges in a significant way on Christian faith
and praxis:

> Instead of recognizing Scripture as a unique and fundamental
> authority, the Church has added to its own ecclesiastical tradi-
> tion, and then extended the ground covered by this tradition
> more and more, until finally the whole life of the Church,
> especially the present life of the Church, came to be regarded
> as tradition. In the course of time the existing Church and its

8

magisterium has come more and more to be taken for tradition. At Trent tradition ousted Scripture, at Vatican I real historical tradition was in turn ousted by the present magisterium of the Church. Trent said that tradition shows what Scripture teaches; Vatican I said that the Church teaches what tradition is. The 'teaching of the Church', understood in this way, and hence the Church itself was made identical with the revelation of Christ.

Such a Church, he continues, 'has no option' but to claim infallibility.[2] This, in fact, is exactly the position officially declared in the *Catechism of the Catholic Church* (1994), in which Scripture and Tradition 'must be accepted and honoured with equal sentiments of devotion and reverence', and only the *magisterium* can authentically interpret 'the Word of God, whether in its written form or in the form of Tradition' (82–85). This is simply unacceptable to most other Christians.

Vatican II had gone some way towards resetting the balance when it observed that the teaching office of the present Church 'is not above the Word of God, but serves it'.[3] Similarly, it affirmed that 'this tradition which comes from the apostles *develops* in the Church with the help of the Holy Spirit'.[4] But there is no suggestion of a limit to this development and the *Constitution* goes on to state that 'sacred tradition and sacred Scripture form one sacred deposit of the Word of God, which is committed to the Church'.[5] This blurs the edges between Scripture and tradition, just as the *Constitution* blurs the distinction between Scripture and the teaching office of 'the successors of the apostles ... led by the Spirit of truth', so that 'consequently, it is not from sacred Scripture alone that the Church draws her certainty about everything which has been revealed'.[6]

While welcoming the advances here one cannot but feel that the basic problem about the status and limits of sacred tradition still remains. Welcome too are the *Constitution*'s references to the Spirit's action in the functioning of the traditionary process. Is it, however, acceptable to group Scripture, tradition and the *magisterium* in an equality of standing? 'Sacred tradition, sacred Scripture, and the teaching authority of the Church ... are so linked and joined together that one cannot stand without the others, and that all together and each in its own way under the action of the one Holy Spirit contribute effectively to the salvation of souls.'[7] The history of Christian doctrinal debate and differences will indicate that there is in fact a hidden agenda here concerning tradition, continuity, development and criteria for authenticity. The Anglican *Articles of Religion* uncover this with a clear-cut limit in the appeal to tradition and by defining the relationship of Church and Scripture. Church and Bible are indissolubly linked, as H. P. Liddon put it long ago: 'We cannot separate the Bible from the Church which recognized and has preserved it. The Divine Book and the Divine Society are the two factors of the one Revelation – each checking the other.'[8] The importance of tradition is not that it is an alternative or even a supplement to Scripture but that it is a means to its interpretation. It shows how the words of Scripture have been understood by the Church. This was why the canon of 1571 directed the clergy not to teach as authoritative anything 'except what is agreeable to the doctrine of the Old and New Testaments, and *what the Catholic Fathers and ancient bishops have collected from the same doctrine*'.[9]

The nature of this essential link and relationship is spelt out in Article XX, where the Church is seen as 'a witness and a keeper of Holy Writ' but also as being under the Word which it proclaims, for 'it is not lawful for the Church to ordain anything that is contrary to God's Word written ... [so that] ... besides the same ought it not to enforce anything to be believed for necessity of Salvation'. Article VI had already declared the primacy of the Scriptures and their sufficiency for Salvation. They are the unique source for the record of the unique revelation. They are 'the real origins' (Küng), the ultimate criterion to decide authenticity. The teaching authority of the Church (*auctoritas*) is limited by Scripture, as are also the decisions of the General Councils of the Church (Article XXI). On the other hand, the Church has

the right (*ius statuendi*) to change 'traditions and ceremonies', provided always 'that nothing be ordained against
God's Word' (Article XXXIV).

In other words, Scripture is decisive in determining the
legitimacy of any doctrine or practice accordingly as the
living tradition of the living Church evolves. The Church is
the interpreter of the Word but is under the Word, just as a
judge is the interpreter of the law but is himself subject to it.
Scripture is the primary check which limits tradition and
controls development. Revelation, as we suggested earlier,
has a dynamic of life, demanding constant re-presentation
and an ever-deepening awareness of its limitless implications,
but always this process is under the check of Holy
Scripture.[10] The living tradition of the living Church in the
past and in the present is, to use Hanson's image in his Tuohy
lectures, like a boat moored to a fixed buoy, Holy Scripture:
'There is a point at which the cable attached to the buoy
always checks its course, not always pulling it back to the
same point, but always preventing it moving any further on
its existing course.'[11] In every age, the Body of Christ (which
is people trying to grasp through grace that they live spiritually
through the Life of Christ Risen transmitted in Word and
Sacrament) is in the world as well as in the Spirit. The
members of the Body are open in every century to societal
and cultural norms and influences, to group-pressures and to
the effects of doctrinal debate and controversy from the
Church in Corinth to the Church of today. A criterion of
authenticity is necessary if 'the faith once for all delivered' is
to maintain its pristine purity as a dynamic controlling interpretation as the living Church through the centuries
proclaims 'the truth in Christ', 'the truth of the gospel', 'the
truth in Jesus', to use the New Testament descriptions. So,
tradition is limited by Scripture and this, in fact, was the
position in the early Church. The Fathers proved the rule of
faith from Scripture. Hanson, in his *Tradition in the Early
Church* (1962), demonstrates that for them tradition was not
an independent authority: 'it is at any rate certain that all the
Fathers believed that the rule of faith was in its contents

identical with the contents of the Bible, and that they all regarded the rule as open to being proved from the Bible'.[12]

In view of the constant Anglican affirmation that the Anglican Church and the Anglican presentation of the Faith are at one in continuity with the Primitive Church and its teaching – 'we are very ready to stand to the award and umpirage of the Primitive Church'[13] – it may serve to round off this section and to lead into the next by noting how Archbishop William Laud handled this complex of Church, Scripture, tradition and reason. Somewhat underrated as a theologian, his policies and his martyrdom claiming the attention of historians, he nevertheless writes for a Church on this fundamental question. 'The ancient Fathers relied upon the Scriptures' and made 'the creed the rule of faith', and this, he holds, is the position of the Church of England. The appeal to antiquity provides the evidence, and basic to it is the affirmation of continuity in doctrine – 'one and the same Church still'.[14] While Scripture is central it could not exist in a vacuum apart from the life of the Church within which it was formed in the first place. Interpretation and what Hooker termed 'intrinsic reasonableness' have their place. In this traditionary process reason is an essential element and Laud insists that 'grace is never placed but in a reasonable creature' and that 'man ... is still apt to search and seek for a reason why he will believe'.[15] Nothing can prevent man from weighing this matter 'at the balance of reason', and the vital function of reason in the threefold appeal is affirmed: 'to the same weights he brings the tradition of the Church, the inward motives in Scripture itself'. In the same way, he contends, the Fathers used arguments from natural reason to convince philosophers of the validity of relying on Scripture.[16]

For Laud, while tradition could never be an independent authority neither could Scripture be considered apart from the Church. Scripture is the authenticating standard but tradition too has its force, though unlike Scripture it is open to reduction or revision: 'the Scripture where 'tis plain should guide the Church; and the Church where there's doubt or difficulty should expound the Scripture; yet so as neither the Scripture should be forced, nor the Church so bound up, as that upon just and further evidence, she may not revise that which in any case hath slipt by her'.[17] In other words, the appeal to tradition is limited by Scripture and by reason. In several places he outlines the living relationship between Scripture and tradition with clarity, as when he writes: 'though they do materially, yet they do not equally confirm the authority either of other. For Scripture doth infallibly confirm the authority of Church traditions *truly so called*: but tradition doth but morally and probably confirm the authority of Scripture.'[18]

As pointed out earlier, underlying the appeal to tradition are questions both of continuity and of authority. Laud insisted that some traditions are 'true and firm, and of great, both authority and use in the Church, as being apostolical, but yet not fundamental in the faith'.[19] Early in the *Conference with Fisher* (1639) he set out the nature of the relationship:

> If the Scripture be the foundation to which we are to go for witness, if there be doubt about the faith, and in which we are to find the thing that is to be believed, as necessary in the faith; we never did, nor never will refuse any tradition that is universal and apostolic for the better exposition of the Scripture; nor any definition of the Church in which she goes to the Scripture for what she teaches; and thrusts nothing as fundamental in the faith upon the world, but what the Scripture fundamentally makes 'materiam credendorum', the substance of that which is so to be believed, whether immediately or expressly in words, or more remotely, where a clear and full deduction draws it out.[20]

The distinctiveness of Anglicanism lies in its preference for an economy of essential doctrine and in a liberality concerning non-fundamentals. Thus Laud affirms that Catholicity is not in a 'narrow conclave' and the purpose of his book is 'to lay open those wider gates of the Catholic Church, confined to no age, time or place; nor knowing any bounds but that faith which was once (and but once for all) delivered to the saints'.[21] Then as now for Anglicans the interplay of the *hapax* with the living continuity is central. For Laud the role of tradition is always important; but it is interpretative and supportive, and the doctrinal position is based 'upon the Scripture, and upon the Primitive Church expounding it'.[22] The appeal to antiquity has for Anglicans two functions: it is faith-guarding and identity-affirming. 'Taking consonancy with the original deposit of faith as the standard it affirms identity with the Early Church in terms of a *living continuity* of faith and order.'[23] William Payne summarized the position simply: 'Let that be accounted the true Church, whose Faith and Doctrine is most conformable and agreeable with the Primitive.'[24]

III

Anglican Formularies, Formulations and Tradition

The appeal to tradition runs through Anglican formularies and is everywhere in classical Anglican theology from Jewel to Waterland and on through the nineteenth century, when Keble and Pusey and their immediate predecessors, the old High Churchmen, come to mind. The great figures in the Anglican story are steeped in the writings of the Fathers. Nevertheless the appeal to tradition is for them always in the context of the threefold appeal to Scripture, tradition and reason. As already indicated, it never stands as an authority in itself alone but in a living relationship within a system of checks and balances, and the bearing of this on our subject is, one hopes, beginning to be apparent.

When, in the *Preamble and Declaration* of 1870, the Church of Ireland declared the pre-eminency of Scripture and affirmed that the Church 'doth continue to profess the faith of Christ as professed by the Primitive Church', rejecting 'innovations in doctrine and worship, whereby the Primitive Faith hath been from time to time defaced or over-laid', it was echoing the theme of the original preface (1549) to the Book of Common Prayer. This preface put Scripture at the centre of the liturgy as well as of doctrinal formulation, and it appeals in this respect to the 'godly and decent order of the ancient Fathers' who so ordered the liturgical reading of Holy Scripture that 'wholesome doctrine' and devotion, 'the love of his true Religion', should be daily promoted and nourished both for the clergy and the laity. The preface insists that 'here you have an order for prayer, and for

15

reading of the holy Scripture, much agreeable to the mind and purpose of the old Fathers'. Similarly, *Concerning Ceremonies* (1549) declares that those who complain that some ancient ceremonies have been retained 'ought rather to have reverence unto them for their antiquity'. The *Preface* of 1662 rejected any proposed alterations which the revisers regarded 'as secretly striking at some established doctrine, or laudable practice of the Church of England, or indeed of the whole Catholick Church of Christ'. When the Irish revisers of the Book of Common Prayer drew up their *Preface* in 1878, they took note of people's 'love and reverence for the Book of Common Prayer in its main substance and chief parts, and confessed that it contained the true doctrine of Christ, and a pure manner and order of Divine Service, according to the holy Scriptures and the practice of the Primitive Church'.

What we are seeing here is the Anglican awareness that Scripture does not exist in a sort of time-proof vacuum but that it is a living force in the living Church which preserves it and which is subject to it. The appeal to antiquity is an integral part of the Anglican ethos. It is not antiquarianism but an appeal to the teaching and practice of the undivided Church. Laud had put it briefly: 'I believe both Scripture and Creed in the same uncorrupted sense which the primitive Church believed them; and am sure that I do so believe them, because I cross not in my belief anything delivered by the primitive Church.'[1] As I suggested earlier, the appeal is both faith-guarding and identity-affirming. Francis White, Bishop of Ely, who like Laud also disputed with 'John Fisher', spelt it out with reference to the products of the traditionary process:

> The Church buildeth her faith and religion upon the Sacred and Canonical Scriptures ... as upon her main and prime foundation. Next unto the Holy Scripture, it relieth upon the consentient testimony and authority of the Bishops and Pastors of the true and ancient Catholic Church ... The Holy Scripture is the fountain and lively spring ... The consentient and unanimous testimony of the true Church of Christ, in the Primitive Ages thereof, is Canalis, a conduit pipe, to derive

and convey to succeeding generations the celestial water contained in Holy Scripture. The first of these, namely the Scripture, is the sovereign authority and for itself worthy of all acceptation. The latter, namely the voice and testimony of the Primitive Church, is a ministerial and subordinate rule and guide, to preserve and direct us in the right understanding of Scripture.

The consequence of this is that 'genuine traditions agreeable to the rule of faith, subservient to piety, consonant with Holy Scripture, derived from apostolical times by a successive current and which have the uniform testimony of pious antiquity, are received and honoured by us'.[2]

A very important distinction made by Anglicans is explicit in this passage and is confirmed by the coupling of Scripture and the Primitive Church as criteria which we have noted in Anglican formularies. It is the distinction between the doctrine of the undivided Church and later 'traditions' spoken of in Article XXXIV, *Of The Traditions of the Church*, which need not be everywhere the same and are changeable by the authority of the Church so long as 'nothing be ordained against God's Word'. In other words, for Anglicans, the teaching of the Primitive Church is something different, a secondary standard of assay after Scripture and consonant with it. The position was succinctly put by Lancelot Andrewes: 'One canon ... two testaments, three creeds, four general councils, five centuries and the series of the Fathers in that period ... determine the boundary of our faith'.[3] This was the problem faced by the *Interim Statement* (*Towards Reconciliation, 1967*) as it commented on the Anglican/Methodist *Report* of 1963.[4] The problem is how to decide what is authentic tradition, and at once the question of criteria arises. The *Statement*, commenting on the relevant section of the *Report*, gives a clear answer which squares with what we have been uncovering: 'only items of tradition which express and elucidate the norm – that is, the apostolic witness to Christ, as the New Testament records it – are of value'. Such items would be the Creeds, the writings of the Fathers, the Councils, and the formularies and liturgies of

Christendom. Tradition has a necessary role to play but 'the products of the traditionary process must be tested by the Scriptures to which they claim to be subservient and wherever they are found deficient they must be reformed'.[5]

There is then a differentiation being made between what White called 'genuine traditions' which are 'the voice and testimony of the Primitive Church, a ministerial and subordinate rule and guide' and all other products of the traditionary process, many of which are acceptable elements in the Church's deepening apprehension of the faith 'once for all delivered'. Is not this what Küng was saying when he distinguished between 'real historical tradition' and what happens when 'the existing Church and its magisterium has come more and more to be taken for tradition'? In fact, this is precisely the point made by William Payne who had written that 'we are very ready to stand to the award and umpirage of the Primitive Church'. He made the distinction perfectly explicit: 'The pretended infallibility of the present Church and the necessity of receiving and believing all that she imposes must be set by, till it appears that it agrees with the doctrine of the Primitive.'[6] This same problem of how to establish what is authentic tradition was handled by Henry Hammond whose writings rejuvenated Anglican apologetic during the Cromwellian régime. In his *Of Fundamentals* (1654) he concluded that the foundation is contained in Scripture and in 'the creeds or confessions of the universal Church'. Then in his *Paraenesis* (1656) he examines the way in which the foundation is transmitted by means of 'apostolical traditions, *such as are truly so*, as well as apostolical writing'. How then do we make sure that a tradition is authentic? 'The way of trial of any tradition, pretended to be Apostolical, whether it be such or no,' says Hammond,

> is by devoting it to the same, or like Fathers, and Councils ... and from hence it follows, that as we of this age have no other way of judging of the Canon of Scripture, or of any book, or chapter, or period contained in it, but by the affirmation and authority of those testifiers in the first ages of the Church, either by their writings, or by the unquestioned relation of others, brought down and made known to us; so are we

> unable to judge of Apostolical traditions unwritten, whether
> this or that doctrine be such or no, unless it be thus by the
> undoubted affirmations of the ancients ... communicated and
> conveyed to us.

With regard to the qualifications of such testimonies, he
holds that 'the resolution will be unquestionable' if it
conforms to the terms laid down by Vincent of Lérins
(constantly cited by Anglican theologians) – universality,
antiquity and consent. The ultimate authenticating factor
for Hammond is the consonance of antiquity with the
'foundation':

> The universal consent of the doctors of the first age, bearing
> testimony that such a doctrine was from the apostles'
> preaching delivered to all churches by them planted, or
> their general conform testimony herein, without any consider-
> able dissenters producible, is, I acknowledge ... authentic or
> worthy of belief, and so hath been made use of by the
> orthodox of all times as sufficient for the rejecting of any new
> doctrine.

Two things are emerging here: namely, that Anglicanism,
which has consistently laid great stress on the appeal to
antiquity as an essential part of its ethos, has maintained that
there are distinct limits to its reach, status and authority; and
that within the appeal there are degrees or gradations in
tradition. Moreover, it always appears that the appeal to the
authority of the Primitive Church is in matters of doctrine.
The Articles, formularies and the consensus of theologians
differentiate between tradition as represented by the
Primitive Church and by traditions. This is by no means to
dismiss the latter but simply to grade their authority and
importance. Hammond was making the same point when in
his discussion of General Councils he suggested:

> We have learned to distinguish between theological verity and
> Catholic Faith: some things we believe to be true, which yet
> pretend not to be any part of that necessary fundamental
> doctrine which was once delivered unto the saints, but are
> offered to our belief upon grounds of reason, which *supposita
> fide*, carry great weight of probability with them, for which yet
> we neither have, nor pretend any divine revelation.[7]

Nor can it ever be forgotten that the Anglican appeal to tradition is seen by its exponents as being made within the context of a living continuity of faith and order between the Church of today and the Primitive Church. The significance of tradition in this sense is that it is the ongoing process of interpretation by which the Church enters ever more deeply into the apprehension of the one truth, flowing on in the life of the Body. We call to mind Olivier Clément's 'living force' and Lossky's 'dynamic process' as descriptions of tradition. Tradition is interpretative no matter which 'degree' of tradition we are discussing. Hans Küng put it this way:

> All other testimony in the tradition of the Church however profound or sublime, can in essence do nothing more than circle round this testimony of God's word, interpret, commentate, explain and apply the original message according to constantly changing historical situations ... . Sacred Scripture is thus the *norma normans* of the Church's tradition, and tradition must be seen as the *norma normata*.[8]

It has been said of Lancelot Andrewes that his appeal to antiquity 'became the norm of Anglican apologetic'.[9] Of course, Parker before him had affirmed it in 1564 in a letter to Sir William Cecil – 'grounding ourselves (as we do) upon the Apostolic doctrine and pure time of the Primitive Church'. Two years earlier it was basic to Jewel's *Apologia Ecclesiae Anglicanae*, so important that Archbishop Bancroft directed that there should be a copy in every parish. Andrewes himself regarded the book as 'truly a Jewel: whoso will may find our doctrine there'.[10] What was important in Andrewes' exposition was the stress on the historical as well as the theological testimony of antiquity – continuity with the Primitive Church was real, not notional or propositional. 'What he desired,' wrote W. H. Ness, 'was to provide a standard within the history of the Church itself, by which the development of doctrine and institutions might be tested.'[11] The standard existing in the early centuries of the undivided Church was historically ascertainable. The first five centuries were when 'the Church was at its best', sufficiently close to 'the time of Christ and the Apostles for its teaching to have escaped corruption'. Andrewes did not visualize a return to the precise conditions of the Primitive Church, nor did he rule out all subsequent developments, provided they are not held to be *de fide*.[12] Moreover, he distinguishes between customs and traditions, the one being concerned with agenda and the other with credenda, but 'no custom ... against Scripture' is to be observed.[13]

His appeal to the tradition is not an exercise in theological antiquarianism but is focused on historically establishing a living doctrinal continuity with the Primitive Church, and this constant preoccupation with historicity in respect of doctrine remains an element in Anglican theological method: 'There is no principal dogma in which we do not agree with the Fathers and they with us.'[14] The fundamental concern of the appeal to tradition is with Catholicity, and he quotes: 'Let that be reckoned Catholic which always obtained everywhere among all, and which always and everywhere and by all was believed.'[15] Yet there is in Andrewes a liberality which led him to mistrust the narrower formulations of later times but which also allowed him to judge the patristic writers critically when necessary. Indeed, Dean Church noted an element of humanism in Andrewes and there is a sense in which he is a theologian of the Renaissance. Side by side run this vivid sense of the *present reality* of continuity with the past and the sense of the necessity of the freedom of reason to differentiate and to assess.[16] From him, from his immediate predecessors and from the many who followed him, there passed into the Anglican bloodstream a marked inheritance which in the mid-eighteenth century was clinically described by Daniel Waterland when he wrote: 'Scripture and antiquity (under the conduct of right reason) are what we ought to abide by.'[17]

In modern times successive Lambeth Conferences have investigated aspects of the status and function of tradition in varying contexts. Lambeth 1948 looked at it in the context of the elements constituting authority in the Church. This authority 'is distributed among Scripture, Tradition, Creeds, the Ministry of the Word and Sacraments, the witness of saints, and the *consensus fidelium*, which is the *continuing experience of the Holy Spirit* through his faithful people in the Church'.[18] Lambeth 1968 examined the matter in terms of 'the inheritance of faith' which is 'an authority of a multiple kind and that, to the different elements which occur in the different strands of this inheritance, different Anglicans attribute different levels of authority'.[19] As has been suggested at the beginning of our investigation, the underlying questions are and always have been about continuity and authority in Christian doctrine and about the degree of authority attaching to tradition. This aspect surfaces in both reports. Thus, for Lambeth 1948, this authority of the Church 'rests on the truth of the Gospel' and reflects 'the richness and historicity of the divine Revelation'. The elements in this authority are 'in organic relation to each other'. They 'check each other' and 'the emphasis of one element over the others may and does change with the changing conditions of the Church', but always Scripture 'is authoritative because it is the unique and classical record of the revelation'. Nevertheless, 'While Scripture therefore remains the ultimate standard of faith, it should be continually interpreted in the context of the Church's life.' One may recall and compare at this point the definition suggested at the beginning of Chapter II, and note also that the Conference was offering in fact a twentieth-century exposition of the position as outlined in classical Anglican theology, in which the role of tradition is *interpretative under the Spirit's guidance, supportive of and conformable to Scripture* – 'ministerial and subordinate' says White.

The Lambeth Conference of 1968 declares that 'This Faith, which is set forth uniquely in the Scriptures, and is summed up in the Catholic Creeds, develops and grows under the guidance of the Holy Spirit within the life of the Church, the Body of Christ.'[20] The context here is not simply faith considered as the *hapax*, 'the deposit', but renewal in faith seen as man's response to God's initiative in Christ: hence the stress on 'develops and grows under the guidance of the Spirit'. One's mind goes back again to Clément's affirmation that tradition in this sense 'is the expression of the Spirit *juvenescens*'. At the same time the Conference is saying that the faith is uniquely set forth in the Scriptures. The point here is surely that revealed truth does not develop and grow but that *we* develop through apprehending it and grow into its inexhaustible riches, into 'the treasures of Jesus'.[21] So, the *Report* goes on: 'our faith is constantly renewed as the Holy Spirit reveals to us, in the environment in which we live, Christ going on before us, changing the world, and calling us to follow him'.[22] In other words, the Faith (with a capital F) does not change but our faith is always open to fresh apprehensions of it: 'The Church always needs a renewed awareness of the Gospel ... a deeper awareness of *the deposit of faith once delivered to the saints*.'[23] We see here a dual stress on the role of the Spirit abiding in the Church, bringing home to its members the implications of the Faith, and on the *hapax* as the central determinant controlling this deepening awareness, this tradition which 'recapitulates past, present and future ... in contemporaneity with the reality of the Gospel' – thus Lossky on tradition as 'a dynamic process'.[24]

As the *Report* emphasizes, 'the Church and Christian tradition cannot truly be themselves if they are static'. Sometimes reformulations have been and are necessary.[25] But always this traditionary process, these reformulations and developments, are subject to what Küng calls the 'unique and fundamental authority' of Scripture. Archbishop Michael Ramsey stated it with simplicity:

> Developments then took place, but they were all tested. The tests of a true development are whether it bears witness to the gospel, whether it expresses the general consciousness of the Christians, and whether it serves the organic unity of the Body in all its parts. These tests are summed up in the Scriptures, wherein the historical gospel and the experience of the redeemed and the nature of the one Body are described. Hence, while the Canon of Scripture is in itself a development, it has a special authority to control and to check the whole field of development in life and doctrine.[26]

Here we have the dual emphasis on Scripture's authority to control the traditionary process and on historicity as a component element in the functioning of authority. Towards the end of his life Ramsey made an illuminating comment which elucidates what we have been saying about the respective emphases of Orthodoxy and of Anglicanism on the nature and limits of tradition: 'The Orthodox show that the concept of timeless tradition is something we in the West might profit from learning about, and Anglicans show that tradition needs to be embodied in a historical world of process, history, and language to a greater extent than the Orthodox may realize.'[27] In the context of the appeal to Scripture, tradition and reason he went on to make a point which has been implicit throughout our survey, a point which, as we shall see, was forcefully stressed by Hooker long before. 'Traditionalism,' he said, 'is not the same thing as the intelligent appeal to tradition', just as 'Scripturalism is not the same thing as the appeal to Holy Scripture', and 'rationalism can be a very evil thing when it involves a worship of reason, and forgets that reason is concerned with great mysteries'.[28]

We return to Lambeth 1968 by way of concluding this section: 'This inheritance of faith is uniquely set forth in the holy Scripture and proclaimed in the Catholic Creeds set in their context of baptismal profession, patristic reasoning and conciliar decision.' The second strand in this inheritance consists of the Anglican formularies, some of which we have been considering. In the third strand, 'as in the Preface to the Prayer Book of 1549, can be discerned the authority given within the Anglican tradition to reason, not least as exercised in historical and philosophical inquiry'. The addendum of the *Report* crystalizes an element persistent in Anglican theology from Hooker onwards: 'To such a threefold inheritance of faith belongs a concept of authority which refuses to insulate itself against the *testing of history and the free action of reason*. It seeks to be a credible authority and therefore is concerned to secure satisfactory historical support and to have its credentials in a shape which corresponds to the requirements of reason.'[29]

What is beginning to emerge as we examine the Anglican appeal to tradition is that, as the Church goes on its pilgrim way under the abiding Spirit, its presentation of the faith by which it lives, its 'traditioning', is always to be authenticated by 'a unique and fundamental authority' (Küng), interpreted 'under the Spirit's guidance' (Lambeth 1948) for changing conditions of history and in such a way that people in every generation can profess their 'Christian allegiance with reasonableness and a good conscience' (Lambeth 1968).

It was concisely put by Jeremy Taylor, for whom reason was a core-value in theology – 'by reason I do not mean a distinct topic, but a transcendent that runs through all topics'. He wrote:

> All these disputes concerning tradition, councils, fathers etc. are not *arguments* against or besides reason, but *contestations* and pretences to the best arguments, and the most certain satisfaction of our reason. But then all these coming into question submit themselves to reason ... so that Scripture, tradition, councils, and fathers are the *evidence* in a question, but reason is the judge.[30]

IV

Anglican Theology, Antiquity and the Fathers

Behind and supporting this position is a great mass of individual patristic scholarship from Jewel to Waterland and continuing on to the present. Hooker and the Carolines were deeply and familiarly read in the Fathers and frequently assessed them critically. It should therefore help to clarify for us the nature and extent of the Anglican appeal to tradition if we see how antiquity was handled by notable theologians from the Anglican past whose doctrinal concern with the faith of the Primitive Church led them to investigate at a profound level the writings of the early period. Archbishop Ussher, for example, had read the whole of the Fathers in nineteen years and his reputation in patristics was high on the Continent, as was that of George Bull whose *Defence of the Nicaean Faith* (1685) received the congratulations of Bossuet and 'the whole clergy of France'.

We are not talking here solely of knowledge of the Fathers and the contents of their works, but also of patristic scholarship. The critical study of the Fathers was a notable feature in the Church of England. There were, for example, Henry Savile's edition of St John Chrysostom's works in 1613 and Patrick Young's edition of I and II Clement in 1633. James Ussher achieved international repute by his *Polycarpii et Ignatii Epistolae* (1644) in which he rescued the original text, so that his edition still stands as establishing the authentic version of the Ignatian epistles. Henry Hammond's *Dissertationes Quatuor* (1651) followed up the work of Ussher and of Voss on these letters, so important as early evidence for monepiscopacy. On the same subject and with great patristic learning John Pearson defended Ussher's redaction in his *Vindiciae Epistolarum S. Ignatii* (1672) when this was attacked by the French Reformed theologian, Jean Daillé.

I have used the word 'critical' advisedly because while regarding the Fathers generally as exemplary exponents of dogmatic purity, the *hapax*, the Anglican scholars did not treat them as oracles, on occasion disagreeing with a Father or pointing out disagreements between Fathers. Because they revered tradition and emphasized continuity in doctrine they refused to throw out the baby with the bath water.

JOHN JEWEL

We can best see how this worked in practice by glancing at some of the better-known Anglican theologians, and inevitably we begin with Jewel, whose *Apologie* is the first essay in Anglican self-understanding. Straight away we meet the central affirmation of the special norm of the Primitive Church in all questions of tradition and doctrinal authority: 'Surely wee have ever judged the primitive Churche of Christes time, of the Apostles, and of the holie Fathers to be the catholique Churche ... nor yet to fix therein the whole meane of our salvation.'[1] The Church of the first centuries mattered most in these questions because changes and corruptions had not yet been experienced. During Jewel's controversy with Thomas Harding we can see that in this whole area (just as later with William Payne and still later with Hans Küng) the fundamental disagreement is whether the early Church or the present Church can be appealed to for the *authority* of tradition. In his attitude to the Church of the first six centuries being a criterion, Jewel was not seeking to recreate artificially the early Church in his own day. This he made clear, as Booty observes, by making 'a distinction between things necessary and things indifferent in the Church of the apostles and doctors'.[2] In other words, doctrine, use and ceremony must be differentiated. So Jewel wrote:

> I must nedes use this distinction, there were sum orders in the Primitive church commaunded by God, and sum other were

devised by men, for the better trayning of the people. Such
orders as were commaunded by God, may not be changed in
any case ... of the other syde, sutche orders as have been
devysed by men may be broken, upon sum good consideration .... In these thynges, I graunte, the examples of the
doctoores, or Apostles, bynde us not. In these thynges it were
an erroure to say we are bound of necessitie to follow the use
of the Primitive church .... But of the other parte, I saye, that
sutche thynges as God hath commaunded precisely by hys
worde maye never bee broken by any custome or consente ...

– and he instances the withholding of the cup from the
laity as the impermissible reversing of such a dominical
tradition.[3]

In other words, the primitive Church and the present
Church are under the Scriptures which test the authority of
all traditions. His attitude to the Fathers is similar: 'Wee
receive not the disputations or Writings of any menne be they
never so catholike, or praise-worthy as we receive the canon-
ical Scriptures; but that, savinge the reverence dewe unto
them, wee may well reprove or refuse some things in their
writings, if ... they have otherwise thought than the Truthe
may bear them.'[4] The Fathers are fallible and their writings
may not be classed with Scripture. Nevertheless they are
frequently admirable and helpful commentators on the
meaning of the Scriptures: 'In this conference and judge-
mente of the Holy Scriptures wee neede often times the
discretion and wisedome of the Learned Fathers. Yet
notwithstandinge maye wee not geve them herein greater
credite, then is convenient, or then they themselves, if it were
offered, woulde receive.'[5]

What Jewel is saying is that Scripture is supreme, the
authenticating criterion of tradition and the guarantor of
legitimate traditions. Men bring to Scripture their reason,
but it is reason aided by the Spirit abiding in the Church. He
is the promised guide who leads into all truth. For Jewel, the
Primitive Church exemplified the Spirit-led Church doctrinally under the Scriptures. One calls to mind words of the
Roman Catholic theologian George Tavard as he looked at
Jewel's thought on this whole subject:

The Spirit has not left the Church without assistance. He has guided men to understand the word of God. Among those who claim to know Scripture, presumption lies in favour of the early centuries. 'The primitive Church, which was under the apostles and martyrs, has evermore been counted the purest of all others without exception' (Jewel). This is grounded in the old idea of a correspondence between the Church and the Gospel. For the Anglican theologians that correspondence was manifest in the early Church. The first centuries set a pattern to be followed ever after. This is the meaning of the Anglican appeal to antiquity. It is an appeal to the Spirit who guided the Fathers in keeping with the Gospel.[6]

Here certainly is a comment which helps to illuminate a major element in the way in which Anglicans understood and used the appeal to tradition.

The whole thrust of the *Apologie* and of the *Defence* was to demonstrate theologically and historically that doctrines and practices such as infallibility and transubstantiation, the withdrawal of the chalice from the laity and compulsory clerical celibacy, are not part of the authentic historical tradition, but innovations. Forty years on, Lancelot Andrewes would be saying the same thing: 'We do not innovate; it may be we renovate what was customary among the ancients'; and he added that, if opinions are new, 'they are not ours. We appeal to antiquity, and to the most extreme antiquity.'[7] This is the position undergirding the Preamble to the Constitution of the Church of Ireland (1870), which 'doth hereby re-affirm its constant witness against all those *innovations* in doctrine and worship, whereby the Primitive Faith hath been from time to time defaced or overlaid'.

RICHARD HOOKER

With his seminal work *The Laws of Ecclesiastical Polity* (1594/7), Richard Hooker brings a stage further the argument in the *Apologie* of his patron Jewel. His book is 'in one sense a defence of reason, an attempt to establish ... a liberal method which holds reason to be competent to deal with questions of ecclesiastical polity and to be itself an ultimate factor in theology'.[8] The *Polity* is a positive and organic presentation of Anglicanism, its faith, order and practice, and in his classic statement of the threefold appeal it is to be noted that Hooker places reason second and tradition third:

> Be it in matter of the one kind or the other, what Scripture doth plainly deliver, to that the first place both of credit and obedience is due; the next whereunto is whatsoever any man can necessarily conclude by force of reason; after these the voice of the Church succeedeth. That which the Church by her ecclesiastical authority shall probably think and define to be true and good, must *in congruity of reason* overrule all other inferior judgments whatsoever.[9]

We note the qualification 'in congruity of reason'.

That is to say, tradition may not be devalued. Hooker revered tradition: 'Neither may we in this case lightly esteem what hath been allowed as fit in the judgment of antiquity, and by the long continued practice of the whole Church; from which unnecessarily to swerve, experience hath never as yet found safe.'[10] Always the control is Scripture, and he issues a warning against those who 'look for new revelations from heaven, or else dangerously add to the word of God uncertain tradition'.[11] Tradition, moreover (and unlike Scripture), is changeable by the authority of the Church. Hooker, like Ramsey after him, is declaring against traditionalism, the dead hand of a fundamentalism of tradition:

> All things cannot be of ancient continuance, which are *expedient* and needful for the ordering of spiritual affairs: but the Church being a body which dieth not hath always power, as occasion requireth, *no less to ordain that which never was*, than to ratify what hath been before ... the Church hath authority to establish that for an order at one time, which at another time it may abolish, and in both do well.[12] (Italics mine.)

In other words, things can happen for the first time and there is such a thing as the unprecedented event. The only exception to this is 'articles concerning doctrine'. As can be seen in the foregoing extracts, Hooker's use of the concept of 'aptness' or 'fitness', what is *expediens*, indicates that all things pertaining to the polity of the Church are open to revision under the guidance of *the Spirit abiding in the Church*. This is brought out in Book III where the key function of reason, but a Spirit-aided reason, is delineated in respect of determining what in this connection is expedient for the Church:

> For this cause therefore we have endeavoured to make it appear, how in the nature of reason itself there is no impediment, but that the self-same Spirit, which revealeth the things that God hath set down in his law, may also be thought to aid and direct men in finding out by the law of reason what laws are expedient to be made for the guiding of his Church, over and besides them that are in Scripture.[13]

Clearly, Hooker is saying that the tradition of the Church in matters not prescribed by Scripture is not an ever-increasing accumulation of irreversible 'traditions' but a transmission process in which reduction and change may have a place as well as acceptance within the Spirit-led community of faith:

> Lest therefore the name of tradition should be offensive to any, considering how far by some it hath been and is abused, we mean by traditions, ordinances made in the prime of Christian religion, established with that authority which Christ hath left to his Church for matters indifferent, and in that consideration requisite to be observed, till like authority see just and reasonable cause to alter them.[14]

Tradition, then, is open to reassessment from time to time within the living continuity of the Church: 'the whole body of the Church hath power to alter, with general consent and upon necessary occasion even the positive laws of the apostles, if there be no command to the contrary, and it manifestly appears to her, that change of times have clearly taken away the very reasons of God's first institution'.[15]

In other words, the Church must be able to entertain the possibility that change may be required and that unprecedented situations can arise. Even more strikingly, Hooker argues that 'the matter of faith is constant, the matter contrariwise of action daily changeable, *especially the matter of action belonging unto church polity*'.[16]

As the sixteenth century melts into the seventeenth, Hooker is the first to spell out in detail the limits in the appeal to tradition, although the realization of these limits is explicit throughout the theology of the succeeding century. The question then arises for our theme whether, given such principles, Hooker could reject the ordination of women had that situation arisen for him? Precisely this question is addressed by Stephen Sykes in an essay on Richard Hooker in his book, *Unashamed Anglicanism* (1995), in which he concludes from passages such as those we have quoted that Hooker's 'new-grown occasion' is upon us with the priestly ordination of women.[17] His thesis is that such ordinations are entirely consistent with Hooker's theological method – and this in spite of Hooker's resistance to the claim that women can be 'ministers in the Church of God'.[18] The fact is that Hooker's thinking was based on the doctrine of women's subordination deriving from Aristotelian medical and ethical theory married to patristic teaching on the Fall, a view 'being undermined, even as he wrote, by the fact of the rule of Queen Elizabeth', by the government of Mary, Queen of Scots, and by that of Catherine de Médicis. Sykes's handling of the material is particularly illuminating in respect of our argument that there are limits to the authority of tradition.

Later in his book (pp. 168–9) he turns to the notion of a distributed authority, as set out by Lambeth 1948 and which we have already discussed. He regards it as a fundamental feature of Anglicanism 'which is anything but a matter of antiquarian interest'. It is a view of authority mediated not in one mode but in several, and dispensed by the episcopate in synodical association with the clergy and laity, and through all is 'the continuing experience of the Holy Spirit through His faithful people in the Church'. The criterion, in other words, is Scripture, tradition and reason mutually checking each other under the guidance of the Spirit abiding in the

Church. Sykes concludes: 'Unless I am very much mistaken, this is the only kind of authority justifiable in the universal Church of Christ, and is one which we as Anglicans have every reason to explore, to expound and to defend, without a hint of that curiously smug self-deprecation which has so paralysed us in our public theological stances of late'. The bearing of this on the circumscribed role of tradition in the mutually checking process of doctrinal authentication is relevant, as is its application to the ordination of women.

One cannot say too clearly, I believe, to some Anglicans and to official Roman Catholicism that their Scripturalism and their Traditionalism will not answer. Fundamentalism in either tends to trip over its own assertions. If the rule forbidding women to teach is permanently binding, why not other rules such as the covered head in Church and the practice of the *agapē*? If the tradition of an all-male ministry cannot be broken, then by what authority was the dominical tradition of the eucharistic cup for all reversed? A hermeneutic of Scripture and of tradition is essential and in one form or another is no newcomer and certainly not in the Anglican tradition. We dare not yield to fundamentalism or to traditionalism since either way we lose the fullness of the Anglican heritage.

Sykes underlines Hooker's sense of the social reality of the Church in time and history, 'being both a society and a society supernatural'.[19] History provides exigencies and emergencies and Hooker insists that a principle of change can be required by 'some new growne occasion'.[20] The core of his argument is that even apostolic ordinances can be changed when the reasons for making them no longer exist. We are obliged to quote again: 'The whole body of the Church hath power to alter, with general consent and upon necessary occasions, even the positive laws of the apostles, if there be no command to the contrary, and it manifestly appears to her, *that change of times have clearly taken away the very reasons of God's first institution.*'[21]

This, of course, goes to the heart of a theological method in which reason, aided and directed by the Spirit, bears on the formulation of tradition and on the interpretation of Scripture and its proper use: 'When that which the word of God doth but deliver *historically* we conster without any warrant as if it were *legally* meant, and so urge it further then we can prove that it was intended, do we not add to the laws of God, and make them in number seem more than they are?'[22] Hooker makes here a statement of great importance and continuing relevance, implying as it does the requirement of a hermeneutic. This, of course, bears acutely on the contention that the *fact* that the twelve apostles were male creates a *law* that the priesthood for all time must be exclusively male.

His general position then is radical, demonstrating that interaction and mutual checking of the elements which are in organic relation within the threefold appeal, as Lambeth 1948 would put it centuries later.[23] It cannot be ignored by Anglicans debating the priestly ordination of women. Sykes's conclusion bears on this:

> It shows Hooker to be the architect of an understanding of church polity which can seriously consider the necessity of change, even in an institution as traditional as an all-male priesthood. It does not, of course, turn Hooker into an advocate of women's ordination. But on his own principles Hooker would undoubtedly have been ready to consider an argument which destroyed the status of the doctrine of women's subordination as a deliverance of natural reason ... when generalised female subordination ceases to make sense medically or empirically, the route must be open for a reappraisal of the scriptural positive law concerning the impropriety of female teachers.[24]

One must interject here that the Scriptural evidence, on the contrary, does provide examples of women teachers. Our conclusion must be that this matter cannot be evaluated by traditionalism or by scripturalism, but by what Ramsey termed the intelligent appeal to Scripture and to tradition within the ongoing life in space and time of the Spirit-led community. Recently, Paul Avis summed it up: 'the place that classical Anglicanism allocates to tradition is then favourable though strictly circumscribed. *Primitive tradition* illuminated the biblical text. The mind of the Fathers was assimilated into the Anglican way of thinking.'[25]

Hooker's veneration for the Fathers was as deep as his knowledge of their writings was extensive. The pages of the *Ecclesiastical Polity* constantly demonstrate the intimacy of his acquaintance with patristic works. Yet the appeal to tradition is limited for Hooker not only by Scripture – 'in Scripture we are taught all things necessary to salvation' – but by reason – 'for it confirmeth me in this my belief the more'. As to how we know that Scripture 'teacheth us that saving truth ... some answer that to learn it we have no other way than only tradition ... but is this enough?' Certainly, agrees Hooker, it is the common experience that 'the first outward motive leading men so to esteem of the Scripture is the authority of God's Church'. For any member to deny this is 'an impudent thing', and the more we ponder on 'the mysteries thereof' the more we find that 'the very thing [i.e. Scripture itself] hath ministered farther reason'. But when the truth of the Faith is questioned, 'this giveth us occasion to sift what reason there is, whereby the testimony of the Church concerning Scripture, and our own persuasion which Scripture itself hath confirmed, may be proved a truth infallible'. Nor can the exponents of the 'tradition-answer' resort to the opinions of the Fathers as conclusive and regulatory: 'In which case the ancient Fathers being often constrained to shew, what warrant they had so much to rely upon the Scriptures, endeavoured still to maintain the authority of the books of God by arguments such as unbelievers themselves must needs think reasonable.' Always for Hooker this reason is 'an instrument which God doth use unto such purposes', the grace of the Holy Spirit 'enlightening our minds'.[26]

As one evaluates Hooker's contribution on the subject of the appeal to tradition Avis's conclusion is just:

> Richard Hooker was the first to formulate on the basis of first principles the typical appeal of classical Anglicanism to scripture, reason (or experience) and tradition (or antiquity). At the hands of the Caroline divines, Hooker's method – albeit with

some differences of emphasis between the liberals such as Hales and Chillingworth who endorsed Hooker's placing of reason above tradition, and the high churchmen who tended to reverse Hooker's order – created the finest flower of Anglican divinity, a monumental theological achievement. Hooker established the place of reason, as competent to interpret Scripture, adjudicate on tradition and instruct the church as to what was and was not binding in both, in Anglican theological method.[27]

JEREMY TAYLOR

By way of illustrating this we may turn to the writings of Jeremy Taylor, arguably one of the most intelligent and undoubtedly the best known today of Hooker's successors. In his theology reason is as vital in function as is the appeal to Scripture and to antiquity. Together with his veneration for the Fathers and his emphasis on the Primitive Church goes what his friend Rust called 'the largeness and freedom of his spirit'. He criticizes those who 'allow us to be Christians and disciples, if we will lay aside our reason, which is that guard of our souls'.[28] Yet, in an age when Anglican theology was saturated with patristics, few made fuller use of tradition and antiquity in setting forth the Church's faith. Always he does so within the context of the threefold appeal, as for episcopacy in *Of the Sacred Order and Offices of Episcopacy* (1642), and as for the theology of the Eucharist in *The Real Presence and Spiritual* (1654), where he writes: 'This thing I will try by Scripture, by reason, by sense, and by tradition.'[29] His moral/ascetical theology, in which subject Taylor was a leading exponent of a restructured moral theology, is similarly based: 'I affirm nothing but upon grounds of Scripture, or universal tradition, or right reason discernible by every disinterested person.'[30]

He writes of the Fathers' 'great reputation, which I desire should be preserved as sacred as it ought'.[31] His contention, however, is to show that the appeal to the Fathers acquits us 'from any other necessity of believing than of such articles as are recorded in Scripture'.[32] We are recalled to the Anglican

insistence that Christian doctrine is authenticated by
Scripture and the Primitive Church affirming and interpreting it. The appeal to the Fathers is then confirmatory
because 'when the Fathers appeal to tradition it is such a
tradition as delivers the fundamental points of Christianity,
which were also recorded in Scripture'.[33] Tradition and the
Fathers do not therefore constitute in themselves an independent, much less an ultimate, authority, though 'there are
some that think they can determine all questions in the world
by two or three sayings of the Fathers, or by the consent of
so many as they will please to call a concurrent testimony'.[34]

It is in the critical modernity of his use of the appeal to
tradition that we see in Taylor the legacy of him whom he
called 'the incomparable Mr Hooker'. More than that we
can see in him the growth of a new historical criticism, the
development of which was notably advanced in a book
published in 1631 by the French Protestant Jean Daillé, and
entitled *Traicté de l'employ des saints pères, pour le jugement
des differends qui sont aujourd'hui en la religion*. He held
that though the Fathers were 'very able and excellent men'
they were subject to error, often disagreeing, and that it was
useless to appeal to them for a consensus. In fact, 'one of the
right uses of them was precisely to show how soon and how
extensively the corruption had spread'.[35] Daillé's work influenced the members of the Tew Circle, Falkland, Chillingworth and Hales, to whom the book gave an impetus by its
claim that antiquity could not provide an agreed and settled
criterion. Falkland, according to Hyde, 'had read all the
Greek and Latin Fathers' but concluded that the appeal to
them led nowhere; and Chillingworth agreed: 'a consent of
Fathers of one age against a consent of Fathers of another
age'.[36] Hyde himself, while accepting 'where the tradition is
as universal or as manifest as it is in that of the Scripture' still
maintains that the Fathers 'were never all of one mind, and
therefore may very lawfully have their reasons examined by
the reasons of other men'.[37] Hales held that it is not 'knowledge of antiquity … nor authority of councils' that resolves
doctrinal questions but 'the plain uncontroversable' part of

Scripture.[38] It would appear that for the Tew Circle the Fathers were a source of references rather than a standard of reference.

Nevertheless, as I have argued elsewhere,[39] although Daillé and the English theologians influenced by him strengthened the critical attitude to 'antiquity', they did not remove or even seriously damage the appeal to tradition and the Fathers as Anglicans used it. The reason for this is that much of Daillé's contention was for them beside the point, since Anglicans had never appealed to a supposed unanimity among the patristic writers but rather to the Fathers appealing to Scripture and to genuine tradition as confirmatory of Scripture. We can see this confirmed by Jeremy Taylor, who was ready to acknowledge his debt to Daillé in respect of method:

> Except it be in the Apostles' Creed, and articles of such nature, there is nothing which may with any colour be called a consent, much less tradition universal. But I will rather choose to shew the uncertainty of this topic by such an argument which was not in the fathers' power to help, such as makes no invasion upon their great reputation, which I desire should be preserved as sacred as it ought. For other things, let who please read M. Daillé 'du Vray Usage des Pères': but I shall only consider that the writings of the fathers have been so corrupted by heretics, so many false books put forth in their names, so many of their writings lost ... and at last an open profession made and a trade of making the fathers speak, not what themselves thought, but what other men pleased ... .[40]

In fact, Taylor's whole thesis in *The Liberty of Prophesying* (1647) is concerning the uncertainty of tradition to expound Scripture, the fallibility of papal exposition, and the inability of the Fathers 'to determine our questions with certainty and truth'. His conclusion is:

> he that follows his own reason, not guided only by natural arguments, but by divine revelation, and all other good means – hath great advantages over him that gives himself wholly to follow any human guide whatsoever, because he follows all their reasons and his own too: he follows them till reason

> leaves them, or till it seems so to him, which is all one to his
> particular; for, by the confession of all sides, an erroneous
> conscience binds him, when a right guide does not bind him.

This is the modernity in Taylor's use of antiquity, and if
Taylor is reckoned by some to be a high churchman we must
qualify Avis's comment that the Caroline high churchmen
tended to reverse the order of reason and tradition.[41] As we
have noted at the close of the preceding section, this is how
Taylor came to his conclusions about tradition and antiquity:
'Scripture, tradition, councils, and fathers, are the evidence
in a question, but reason is the judge.'[42]

Evidently Taylor was sensitive to the suggestion that he
had not been evenhanded in his use of the appeal to tradition. When, in 1657, his *Liberty of Prophesying* (1647), his
Episcopacy Asserted (1642) and his *Apology for Authorized
and Set Forms of Liturgie* (1649) were reissued as a single
volume, he felt impelled to explain his position in a second
dedication to his friend Sir Christopher Hatton:

> But I have been told, that my discourse of episcopacy, relying
> so much upon the authority of fathers and councils, whose
> authority I so much diminish in my liberty of prophesying, I
> seem to pull down with one hand what I build with the other:
> to these men I am used to answer ... if I had wholly destroyed
> the topic of ecclesiastical antiquity, which is but an outward
> guard of episcopacy, to preserve the whole ecclesiastical order,
> I might have been too zealous ... but I have done nothing of
> this, as they mistake. For episcopacy relies, not upon the
> authority of fathers and councils, but upon Scripture, upon the
> institution of Christ, or the institution of the apostles, upon an
> universal tradition, and an universal practice, not upon the
> words and opinions of doctors.[43]

Leaving to one side the common simplification of
seventeenth-century apologists for episcopacy – the Council
of Trent agreed with Taylor that the threefold ministry was
'by divine ordinance' but Vatican II claimed that it was 'ab
antiquo'[44] – what is to be noted here is the usual Anglican
emphasis on a universal tradition, made even by the
members of the Tew Circle. The critical veneration for the

Fathers which is observable in Anglican writings from Jewel onwards is fully expressed by Taylor in the *Dedication* to demonstrate what Michael Ramsey termed 'the intelligent appeal to tradition': 'as the probability of it can be used to one effect, so the fallibility of it is also of use to another'. Taylor then proceeds to spell this out:

> he that says, that in questions of religion, the sayings of the fathers alone is no demonstration of faith, does not speak things contradictory. He that says that we may dissent from the fathers, when we have a reason greater than that authority, does no way oppose him that says, you ought not to dissent from what they say, when you have no reason great enough to outweigh it. He that says the words of the fathers are not sufficient to determine a nice question, stands not against him, who says they *are excellent corroboratives* in a question already determined and practised accordingly. He that says, the sayings of fathers are no demonstration in a question may say true; and yet he that says, it is a degree of probability, may say true too. He that says they are not our masters, speaks consonantly to the words of Christ; but he that denies them to be good instructors, *does not speak agreeably to reason or to the sense of the church*. Sometimes they are excellent arbitrators, but not always good judges: in *matters of fact* they are excellent witnesses; in matters of right or question they are rare doctors, and because they bring good arguments, are to be valued accordingly.[45]

Taylor himself took just such an independent line in respect of some of St Augustine's teaching on original sin: 'his zeal against a certain error made him take in auxiliaries from an uncertain or less discerned one and caused him to say many things which all antiquity before him disowned and which the following ages took up upon his account'.[46] His opposition to the contemporary Augustinianism in his *Unum Necessarium* (1655) cost him some friends, but he would not retract because so many of these propositions were in his view against Scripture and reason: 'Could we prevent the sin of Adam? Could we hinder it? Were we ever asked?'[47] Finally, we discern in Taylor's handling of the appeal to tradition the distinction between the appeal to the

Primitive Church and the status of other instances of the appeal: 'I have a great reverence for antiquity, *yet it is the prime antiquity of the Church*, the ages of martyrs and holiness that I mean; and I am sure that in them my opinion hath much more warrant than the contrary.'[48]

Nor need it surprise us to find instances of Anglicans of the classic period turning the appeal to antiquity back on their own Church. Herbert Thorndike (1598–1672) for example, insists that in appealing to antiquity the Church of England 'had not in all points carried out her own principle': and he instances penance and discipline (as recommended by the Prayer Book), prayer for the departed, the *epiclesis* in the Eucharist, and presbyters as a council with the bishop, pretty well all of which are now restored among the Anglican Churches. For Thorndike, a vigorous and influential Anglican apologist not silenced by deprivation under the Commonwealth, the fundamental theme in his works such as *Just Weights and Measures* (1662) and *Of the Government of Churches* (1641) is that conformity to the Primitive Church is basic. It is the familiar Anglican emphasis on the especial value and standing of the 'primitive' in the establishing and ascertaining of authentic doctrine. William Payne put the viewpoint in a nutshell, as we have quoted before: 'Let that be accounted the true Church, whose Faith and Doctrine is most conformable and agreeable with the Primitive.'[49]

SIMON PATRICK

Towards the close of the century, Simon Patrick (1626–1707) was a leader in the new generation of Restoration clergy whose example, practice and writings did so much for the devotional, eucharistic and theological life of the Church in a changing society. Two elements combine in Patrick to produce a rounded exposition of Anglicanism, a liberality of outlook and an active awareness of the Church as the living embodiment of its own past. Antiquity is a standard of reference in the past, but it is also a continuing formative element in the present.

Having learnt from the Cambridge Platonists to oppose 'the hide-bound spirit', he rejects 'absolute reprobation' and insists that the faith that justifies is faith 'which works by love'. Those who share his position do not look to the Schoolmen, or 'Dutch systematics', to the Council of Trent or to the Synod of Dort, but to 'the writings of the apostles and evangelists, in interpreting whereof, they carefully *attend to the sense of the ancient Church*, by which they conceive the modern ought to be guided: and therefore they are very conversant in all the genuine monuments of the ancient fathers, those especially of the first and purest ages'.[50] In his *Brief Account* (1662) and his *Friendly Debate* (1668) he welcomes the current advances of science, 'the new philosophy', and central to his thought is a restatement of the threefold appeal. Things cannot be believed unless there be a reason, which may be 'a deduction from the light of nature, and those principles which are the candle of the Lord', *or* revelation in Scripture, *or* 'the general interpretation of genuine antiquity', *or* 'lastly the result of some or all of these'. Reason requires taking 'all that is reasonable into consideration'. He had 'a profound reverence' for Smith, the Cambridge Platonist, who influenced Patrick at Queens' College, Cambridge, and reason as the candle of the Lord lights his work. Yet with this emphasis on reason and experience Patrick combines an active acceptance of the implications of the historicity of the Church for doing theology and for authenticating doctrine. He will go so far as to affirm, 'nor is there any point in divinity, where that which is most ancient doth not prove the most rational'. The same point is made when he defends his teachers and colleagues: 'Let no man accuse them of hearkening too much to their own reason, since their reason steers by so excellent a compass, the ancient fathers and councils of the Church.'

In Patrick we see Anglicanism determined to proclaim the Faith with openness and liberality but firmly anchored in Scripture and antiquity, and this in a transitional society where as old idols were falling new problems and new

knowledge were fast accumulating. This is both the motiva-
tion and the practicality of what he is saying, because as a
pastor he is deeply concerned in his writings with making the
present Church spiritually and intellectually an effective
force in that society. His awareness of the Church as
embodying its own past is very noticeable in his *Discourse
about Tradition* (1683) as is his stress on reason and on the
hapax, 'the faith once for all delivered', both of which determine the authenticity of a tradition. The Church, Patrick
maintains, does not refuse to accept something delivered
because it is unwritten, but rather it questions the nature and
extent of the authority which so delivers it. This is the basis
of the refusal to accept as tradition anything that adds to the
necessary articles of faith originally delivered. Always, as
suggested in our first chapter, it comes down to questions of
authority and authenticity. He writes that 'the Scripture itself
is a tradition; and we admit all other traditions which are
subordinate and are *agreeable* unto that; together with all
those things which can be proved to be apostolical by the
general testimony of the Church in all ages'. Instances he
offers are infant baptism and the authority of bishops over
presbyters, and this he terms 'confirming tradition'.

Underlying all Patrick writes on the subject are the appeals
to the Primitive Church and the Vincentian canon: the
consensus of the Church 'must be acknowledged also to be of
greater or lesser authority, as it was nearer or farther off from
the time of the apostles'. The unanimous tradition of the
Church, determining the meaning and sense of Scripture,
adds nothing new and is in the nature of an unfolding and an
explanation; and the same may be said of the decrees of the
first four general councils, thus excluding doctrinal innovations. As to any traditions not possessing the same authority,
he holds that reason uses four tests in assessing their value:
where they come from, their content, their authority, and the
means there are of ascertaining whether they are what they
claim to be. We see in Patrick's treatment of the subject an
instance of the growing awareness of the need for a critical
handling of evidence. Kenneth Stevenson's recent evaluation

of him is a concise picture: 'He was, essentially, a man who looked with reason on tradition and Scripture.' Like Jeremy Taylor, he respected tradition but realized its limits: 'both want to be faithful to tradition, but to use their powers of reason to interpret that tradition'.[51] Again and again it is brought home to us that classical Anglicanism rejected traditionalism and employed consistently a hermeneutic of tradition.

V

The Appeal to Antiquity and Tradition in the Eighteenth and Nineteenth Centuries

The work of William Wake (1657–1737) bridges the transition to the new century. As Archbishop of Canterbury his correspondence on Christian unity with the Roman Catholic Gallicans du Pin and Girardin and with the Reformed theologians Jablonski and Turretini showed him to be an ecumenist ahead of his time. Wake, as may be seen in the magisterial study by the late Norman Sykes, was an able, clearsighted and extremely perceptive theologian acutely aware of the bearing of our subject on any effective process of reconciliation between the separated Churches.[1]

It is a fascinating story and, as with his predecessors, Wake's starting point is to invite his correspondent du Pin to note the similarity of the Church of England to the Primitive Church 'cum constitutione, fide, regimine ecclesiae catholicae secundi, tertii aut etiam quarti seculi'. Moreover, Anglicans have preserved and possess 'that ancient and clearly apostolic system' (episcopacy) and 'the ancient creeds of the Catholic Church ... and since in these matters we all agree, in others we ought surely to bear with one another'.[2] This at once brings up what the *Malta Report*, 6 (1968) calls the characteristic Anglican distinction between fundamentals and non-fundamentals, raised as basic by Charles Gore at the Malines Conversations three centuries later: 'the demand for the distinction will go on'.[3] Writing to Turretini, Wake insisted:

45

> that the peace of Christendom can no way be restored but by separating the *fundamental articles* of our religion (in which almost all churches do agree) from others, which in their several natures *though not strictly fundamental*, may yet be of more, or less, moment to us in the way of our salvation ... and ... the first being absolutely provided for, and *the others which are nearest to them, as much secured as conveniently can be done*, communion should not be broken for the rest, but a prudent liberty be granted to Christians to enjoy their own opinions, without censuring or condemning any that differ from them.[4]

Here is an exact and sophisticated setting out of the rationale of this distinction. It is no mere casual drawing of a line with fundamentals obligatory on one side and a free-for-all on the other. Rather is it a question of the nearness to or distance from the fundamentals which decides the importance of 'the others'. Strikingly, though it is not an exact parallel, the Second Vatican Council's decree on ecumenism (11) reads: 'When comparing doctrines, they should remember that in Catholic teaching there exists an order or "hierarchy" of truths, since they vary in their relationship to the foundation of the Christian faith.' The bearing of this on the subject can be seen when his Roman Catholic correspondent du Pin sent his *Commonitorium* to Wake, agreeing 'in regard both to those things necessary to be believed and to those which are indifferent or which can be discussed in either sense without affecting the faith'.[5] Wake was anything but naive as a theologian and he faced the question still being asked – as, for example, in the report of the doctrine commission *Believing in the Church* (1981) – 'Where is doctrine to be found?' He was careful and far from simplistic in his handling of the distinction in a letter to the Roman Catholic theologian, Piers de Girardin:

> You have remembered rightly and wisely that in treating of *articles of evangelical doctrine*, fundamentals should be carefully distinguished from non-essentials ... lest by a promiscuous treatment of these issues any occasion should be given to the incautious of deceiving themselves, as if the chief point of all religion turned on those things .... Neither ought the

peace of the Church to be entirely broken for articles of this nature. It is indeed a work of greater difficulty, not to say danger, to distinguish the essential articles of doctrine from the rest, in such wise that nothing in them is either superfluous or lacking; that nothing essential to salvation is omitted, nor anything non-essential included in the number of essentials.[6]

Wake's general position is clear. In reply to a letter from Quinot he stated that the fundamentals of faith are 'clearly revealed in holy Scripture ... [and] ... in the articles of the three creeds ... these sufficed to define the catholic faith in the first five centuries of the Church'.[7] In his *Exposition of the Articles* (1686) he had affirmed the Scripture 'to be the last resort, the final, infallible rule, by which both we and the church itself must be directed'. Nevertheless, he is far from discounting the authority of tradition, 'rightly established and interpreted'. This proper authority is recognized by the Church of England:

> We receive with the same veneration whatsoever comes from the apostles, whether by Scripture or tradition, *provided that we can be assured that it comes from them.* And if it can be made appear that any tradition which the written Word contains not, has been received by all churches, and in all ages, we are ready to embrace it, as coming from the apostles.

This is the familiar Anglican combination of the Vincentian rule and the standard of the Primitive Church with the Scripture over all: 'whatever other churches adhere firmly to the Vincentian rule, the Church of England is pre-eminent amongst them' (letter to du Pin). Wake accordingly insists that 'Our Church rejects not tradition, but only those things which they [the Roman Catholics] pretend to have received by it; but which we suppose to be so far from being the doctrine of the apostles, or of all churches in all ages, that we are persuaded they are many of them directly contrary to the Written Word.'

Finally, Wake, like his successor Michael Ramsey, agrees that the Scriptures were 'traditioned' by the Church though 'we receive and submit to [them], as to the Word of God':

> The Church, i.e. the universal church in all ages, having
> been established by God, the guardian of the holy scripture
> and of tradition, we receive from her the canonical books of
> scripture .... This authority therefore we freely allow the
> church, that by her hands in the succession of the several ages,
> we have received the holy scriptures. And if as universal and
> uncontroverted a tradition had descended for the interpreta-
> tion of the scriptures, as for the receiving of them, we should
> have been as ready to accept of that too. Such a declaration of
> the sense of holy scripture as had been received by all churches
> in all ages, the Church of England would never refuse.[8]

There is, then, from Jewel to Wake and onwards an
Anglican consensus on the nature of tradition, the levels of it,
the use of it and the limits in appealing to its authority. At the
same time there is a genuine veneration (to use Wake's word)
for tradition properly so called, for its importance in the
continuity of the Church's proclamation of faith. This, as we
have seen, is particularly to be noted in the Anglican respect
for the Fathers as illustrative of and supportive of the appeal
to the Primitive Church. They are evidence of 'how exactly
our Church does in this particular resemble the Primitive,
perhaps beyond any other at this day in the world'. The
words are Wake's and they come from his book *The Genuine
Epistles of the Apostolical Fathers* which he had published in
1693, the year in which he became Rector of St James's,
Westminster. Though it was not, nor was it intended to be, a
work in the same class as the great patristic studies of Ussher,
Voss and Pearson, the book was still 'the first of its kind', to
use Wake's own description. It was in fact a translation – he
writes of 'the drudgery of a translator' – designed to put
before an ordinary intelligent enquirer a selection which
would show the Fathers as authoritative interpreters of
Scripture, and which would demonstrate the validity of
the Anglican appeal to the Primitive Church. Wake's book
was successful in its purpose and it went into a second
edition in 1710.[9]

In effect, Wake's view concerning the authority of tradition
is that Scripture is 'the final, infallible rule', and the appeal
to the Primitive Church confirming this is of superior

authority to any other tradition, however worthy, which is not traceable to either source. Involved with, and indeed an integral element in the application of this appeal, is the characteristic Anglican distinction (going back to Jewel, Whitgift and Hooker) between fundamentals and non-fundamentals. The latter, when authentic, may have their own importance but may not be treated as essential, their importance being decided by their nearness to fundamentals. William Wake was the first to bring this total Anglican ethos in doctrine, spirituality and liturgy into contact and dialogue with representative theologians of the Reformed and the Roman Catholic Churches in terms of the quest for unity in diversity, 'saving on both sides the faith and verity of the catholic church'. The position could hardly be put more clearly than it was by one of Wake's modern successors, Archbishop Runcie of Canterbury, speaking in Westminster Abbey in 1981: 'It is the achievement of unity in diversity through the distinction of the essential from the non-essential by means of the Holy Scriptures interpreted by Tradition, in the light of Reason, all expressed in and through the corporate worship of the Church.' The Anglican ethos has not changed.

In that ethos, 'the intelligent appeal' to antiquity and tradition has been a continuing element despite the efforts of the Tractarians and their subsequent chroniclers to claim that in respect of the appeal there was a gap between the Caroline 'golden age' and their own as marked by their *Library of the Fathers* (1838). H. P. Liddon is typical in his account of the setting up of this project: 'In the seventeenth century her divines were as conversant with them [i.e. the Fathers] as any theologians in Europe, but the Fathers were gradually forgotten as the eighteenth century advanced.' [10] That this was far from being the case has been richly documented by Peter Nockles in his study of Anglican High Churchmanship, 1760–1857, *The Oxford Movement in Context* (1994). He notes that: 'Numerous editions and commentaries on the Fathers poured from the university presses in the three or four decades prior to the rise of

Tractarianism. Works by Daubeny, Cleaver, Van Mildert, John Jebb, Routh, Hawkins, Kaye and Edward Burton in this period, stood squarely within the Caroline tradition of theological method and patristic learning.' This was in spite of 'a decline in deference to antiquity among Hanoverian divines .... Nevertheless Georgian Anglicanism continued to value the Fathers.'[11]

For those whom Nockles calls the old High Churchmen with their repeated insistence on the Vincentian rule,

> the appeal to antiquity could not supersede that which the Reformers and seventeenth-century divines had already made and which had been enshrined in the Church's authorised formularies. The guiding principle of their approach remained *the distinction between fundamentals and non-fundamentals in doctrine and worship*. As Van Mildert (in 1815) explained, Holy Scripture was 'the only Rule of Faith: and whatever benefit may be derived from other writings, reporting to us, as apostolical traditions, additional matters illustrative of our faith and worship; to them is to be assigned no more than *a secondary rank*, as being subsidiary, not essential to our Creed' [Italics mine].[12]

Nockles' book places the Oxford Movement firmly within a continuous and varied High Church tradition in a way that has not previously been attempted. It is a truly indispensable study, revealing the relationship between the old High Churchmen and the Caroline divines and the divergent approach to and use of the appeal to antiquity as between these and the Tractarians who, at the outset of the Movement, felt themselves to be the true heirs of the Carolines, though later they were disappointed with what they saw as seventeenth-century 'reserve' in respect of the appeal to antiquity. This dissatisfaction, however, arose from the Tractarian treatment of the appeal to antiquity as an absolute standard which 'confounded with the acceptable first class of doctrines the equal necessity of other doctrines and practices which had never been considered as binding'.[13] In other words, they ignored the fundamentals/secondary distinction which was the guiding principle of the appeal to tradition for the Carolines and Old High Churchmen alike. Our concern here, however, is simply to underline the continuity of the appeal in the Church of England and to suggest to Anglicans today that the appeal to tradition which may not be separated from the appeal to Scripture and the appeal to reason is a rich inheritance. It comes as no surprise to see this set out in the preliminary booklet *Lambeth 1998*:

> Anglicans uphold the Catholic and Apostolic faith as it was set forth in the Book of Common Prayer and as it has developed in each Church. Within this definition of faith are three pillars: the uniqueness and sufficiency of the Bible, the authority of the early Church in understanding the Bible, and the value of continued study of the Bible for new insights in each generation. The Lambeth Conference expects evolution in Christian thought ...

VI

Some Conclusions

What conclusions are then to be drawn from this survey of the appeal to tradition as an integral element in the Anglican ethos? Passing in review the formularies, formulations and theological works which we have been examining, it is evident that Avis was correct in his judgment that classical Anglicanism gives to tradition a ranking that is favourable though strictly circumscribed.[1] When we turn to the specifics of this circumscription the material we have been assessing shows these certain clear limits in the appeal to tradition. This is never treated as an authority on its own but is an element, and an important one, in the threefold appeal to Scripture, antiquity and reason.

While Scripture itself has been 'traditioned' it stands, by reason of its unique character, as the test of true developments and traditions. It has, as Ramsey noted, 'a special authority to control and check the whole field of development in life and doctrine'. It controls the traditionary process but it does not exist in a vacuum. Scripture exists within the living Church, the recipient of the revelation, which is the community of faith 'in which the pure Word of God is preached, and the Sacraments be duly administered according to Christ's ordinance' (Article XIX). The Church is 'a witness and a keeper of holy Writ', having authority in controversies of faith but is itself under the authority of the Word which controls its determinations concerning the Faith (Article XX). We may have here an echo of the patristic idea of the mutual coinherence of the Scriptures and the Church, a correlation underlying the constant Anglican appeal to the Primitive Church expounding Scripture which as Laud insisted is a criterion for authentic doctrine and saving faith.[2] We recall Tavard's comment that this correspondence between the Church and the Gospel was seen by Anglicans as manifest in the early Church and was the meaning of their appeal to antiquity: 'It is an appeal to the Spirit who guided the Fathers in keeping with the Gospel.' The relationship was not understood by Anglicans to be a simple symbiosis but a living relationship in which the Church and tradition interpret Scripture, itself the ultimate court of appeal in matters of faith. There is something of this in the phrase so important for the Tractarians in respect of the relation of Scripture and tradition – 'the Church to teach and the Bible to prove'. We have seen how Laud had understood the Church/Scripture coinherence when he wrote that 'the Scripture where 'tis plain should guide the Church; and the Church where there's doubt or difficulty should expound the Scripture'. He was equally clear as to the Scripture/Tradition relationship: 'Scripture doth infallibly confirm the authority of Church traditions truly so called: but tradition doth but morally and probably confirm the authority of Scripture.'

We can see in a modern instance how this appeal to Scripture, to the Primitive Church, to tradition and to reason works out. In 1950, when the Dogma of the Assumption was promulgated, a pastoral letter was issued by the bishops of the Church of Ireland. The dogma, they affirm, rests 'on no scriptural authority or historical evidence, and not even on any support from the writings of the most ancient fathers'. The letter goes into some detail, tracing the belief in the first instance to 'an imaginative Oriental document of the fourth century, known as *On the passing of the Virgin Mary*, and classed as apocryphal in a decree attributed to Pope Gelasius'. Dealing with the absence of Scriptural evidence for the Assumption, the unique place of Mary is acknowledged: 'She stands solitary in the mysterious privilege with which she was favoured. It can be shared by no other.' The letter discusses 'Theotokos' and 'Deipara' and comments that 'high honour is due, and rendered' to Mary; but the dogma of 1950 stands as an *innovation* over against 'the ancient Rule of Faith and the primitive Church Order'. In support of the appeal to Scripture and the Primitive Church, the Irish bishops observed:

Pope Benedict XIV stated in 1740 that the most ancient fathers of the Primitive Church are silent as to the Bodily Assumption of the Blessed Virgin; while the same Pope wrote that the Assumption of the Blessed Virgin is not an Article of Faith, seeing that certain passages of Scripture which are wont to be adduced in support of the opinion can be otherwise explained, and that the tradition is not of such a kind as to be sufficient for the elevation of this doctrine to the rank of Article of Faith.[3]

The letter perfectly illustrates the Church/Scripture/Tradition relationship as this is set out in Articles XIX and XX. It is what John Bramhall meant when he wrote: 'Thou art for tradition, so am I. But my tradition is not the tradition of one particular Church contradicted by the tradition of another Church, but the universal and perpetual tradition of the Christian world united. Such a tradition is a full proof, which is received semper, ubique et ab omnibus.'[4] The contemporary letter is simply applying the Anglican synthesis concerning authenticity of doctrine, as outlined, for example, two centuries before by Waterland in *The Use and Value of Antiquity with Respect to Controversies of Faith* which, just as does the Irish bishops' letter, rejects the 'various enlargements' of the Creed by Pope Pius IV as innovations added to the faith of the early Church.[5] Paul Avis comments that 'Waterland upholds the paramount authority of Scripture and looks to the guidance of the early church where scripture itself is unclear.' To this point he adds that 'Waterland has little time for catholic consent as a criterion, except when it is the consent of antiquity.'[6] This is borne out for the whole range of Anglican thinking by our investigation hitherto. Similarly, we find our contention that the appeal to the Primitive Church is in respect of the fundamentals of doctrine continued and confirmed by Waterland: 'the subordinate proof from antiquity may be a good mark of direction for the interpretation of scripture *in the prime doctrines*'.[7] In the introduction to his major work, the *Review of the Doctrine of the Eucharist*, he makes the general affirmation – he was widely read in patristics – that 'great regard ...

ought to be paid to the known sense and judgment of the apostolical Fathers'.

It is, however, I would suggest, in his perceptive comment on the Scripture/tradition/Church area that, like Payne before him and Küng after him, Waterland puts his finger on the nub of the continuing problem:

> If there be any church now in the world which truly reverences antiquity and pays a proper regard to it, it is this church. The Romanists talk of antiquity, while we observe and follow it. For with them, both scripture and fathers are, as to the sense, under the correction and control of the present church: with us, the present church says nothing but under the direction of scripture and antiquity taken together, one as the rule, and the other as the pattern or interpreter.

It is the distinction pressed by Chillingworth in 1637: 'But the tradition of all ages is one thing; and the authority of the present church ... is another.' [8]

This whole area of doctrinal authority and authentication, criteria and development, has been recently described as a minefield. It is the thrust of our investigation into Anglican thinking that this is so only when the distinctions between the respective authority of Scripture, of tradition and of the teaching Church are blurred. Thirty years ago the Roman Catholic position was delineated by George H. Tavard, and the situation would not seem to have changed substantially. Referring to current Roman Catholic manuals, he writes:

> Tradition is called 'passive' or 'active'. Passive Tradition is the content of doctrine: it is the Catholic doctrine as transmitted by the Church. As such, it may denote the entire Christian doctrine. Or it may also refer, in a restrictive sense, only to the points of doctrine that are not made explicit in Holy Scripture. Active Tradition is, first, the act of transmitting doctrine. Basically, this is identical with the apostolic *kerygma*, the preaching of the good news which began with the Apostles and is continued by their successors the bishops. It is also, therefore, secondly, the organ of transmission, namely, the living *magisterium* of the episcopal college under the primacy of the Apostolic See of Rome. Passive and active tradition thus

coincide: in final analysis, the Tradition which the Catholic faith recognizes to be binding in conscience is no other than the Church's very life and its doctrinal implications.[9]

The template used here is flawed in its composition. What is part of the problem of tradition has been incorporated as part of the definition of tradition. The logical conclusion or, as Küng put it, 'the only option', is infallibility, which is doctrinally unacceptable to the Anglican, Orthodox and Reformed Churches on the grounds which we have been considering – Scripture, antiquity and reason.

For Waterland, the appeal to antiquity acts as a control on doctrinal innovations, the point earlier stressed by Andrewes and others, and always there is the appeal to reason: 'I follow the fathers as far as reason requires and no further.'[10] His conclusion is the Anglican synthesis: 'Scripture and antiquity (under the conduct of right reason)' – these are the standard of assay for authentic Christian doctrine.[11] Again, we are looking at a hermeneutic of Scripture and tradition which is an essential element in Anglican theological method. Stevenson's comment that Patrick looked with reason on tradition and scripture comes to mind as a compressed characterization of that method. Archbishop Runcie's definition reminds us that it is a continuing and quintessential constituent therein.

There is a balance in Anglicanism in which, while 'The tradition criticizes us ... we have also to criticize the tradition, drawing upon the best intellectual and moral insights of our own day'. Anglicanism historically has tended to follow tradition unless a good reason can be given for not doing so. In the Anglican synthesis 'reason can be characterized negatively as a counterpoise to unreasoning biblicism or traditionalism'.[12] Hooker and Taylor spring to mind in each respect. The appeal to tradition is a guideline 'to avert mere arbitrariness and individualism in interpretation', as Henry Chadwick has observed, pointing out how the community 'provides the framework of principles within which and from which reason operates'. He continues that within the community of believers 'reason is never properly set in stark antithesis to authority as if the latter were always inscrutable and arbitrary. Reason is neither a subordinate handmaid always submissive to its dogmatic teacher, nor a dangerous harlot ready to seduce, but rather a great gift of God for the understanding of the faith and of the proportion and coherence of its various elements.' [13] Readers of *The Ecclesiastical Polity* will feel that these comments might well be taken *en passant* as a bird's-eye view of Hooker.

As to where we are today, the Anglican heritage from the past is valid currency – reason, never divorced from Scripture or apostolical Tradition, sets us free from fundamentalism, traditionalism and theological idiosyncrasy. This is as true now as it was when Jeremy Taylor affirmed that Scripture, tradition and councils provide the evidence but 'reason is the judge'.[14] Or, as we read in *Celebrating the Anglican Way* (1996):

> Anglicans often speak about the threefold cord of Scripture, reason and tradition. Scripture contains the elements which it is necessary to believe to be a Christian. Reason comprehends our experience as human beings who think and feel and act. Tradition is the reach of the past into the present: the way in which we inherit from the past the experience and knowledge of others who have shared our belief.[15]

In the same collection a comment on the Anglican way of receiving the Scriptures bears on our study here:

> A word needs to be said about the use of reason in the interpretation of Scripture. Against certain radical puritans ... it was argued that only reason could enable you to differentiate between various kinds of material in the Scriptures. Discovery and rational argument were necessary in establishing what could and should be defended as the right way for the contemporary Church.[16]

While this is in effect saying no more than was said in the past by the theologians we have been studying, it does raise a question in respect of our investigation of classical Anglicanism as to the nature and quality of their appeal to Scripture.

The question is this: given the universal attitude to the Biblical text in the sixteenth and seventeenth centuries, were not these theologians fundamentalist in their view of Scripture? That an unqualified or simplistic answer is not possible becomes apparent once we come to look at examples where we are confronted with a hermeneutic at work in company with a belief in the divine authorship of Scripture. Constantly we are being reminded that the Spirit who abides in the Church inspired the written Word and continues to wake it to life, corporately for the household of faith and individually for its members, by the ministry of the Word and Sacraments. It is here, in the process of reception and interpretation, that reason enters as 'a great gift of God for the understanding of the faith and of the proportion and coherence of its various elements'.

There comes to mind Robert Boyle with a European reputation as 'the Father of Chemistry', a devout Anglican who began every day with meditation and prayer. In his *Some Considerations touching the Style of the Holy Scriptures* (1661), he wrote: 'We should carefully distinguish betwixt what the Scripture itself says and what is only said in Scripture. For we must not look upon the Bible as an oration of God to man, or a body of laws like our English Statute Book, wherein it is the legislator that all the way speaks to the people, but as a collection of composures of very different sorts and written at very distant times; and of such composures that though the holy men of God ... were acted by the Holy Spirit, Who both excited and assisted them in penning the Scripture, yet there are many others besides the Author and the penmen introduced speaking there.'[17]

VII

Scripture and Reason (I)

When we look back to Richard Hooker we see this combination in a methodology in which reason plays a significant part, and in an exegesis which sees different levels in Scripture and thus qualifies current ideas on 'total inspiration'. His starting point is 'that the absolute perfection of Scripture is seen by relation unto that end whereto it tendeth'. This is central and, if disregarded, 'racking and stretching it ... so that in Scripture all things lawful to be done must needs be contained' – the Puritan position – this leads to Scripture becoming 'a snare and a torment to weak consciences'.[1] Right reason, reason aided by the Spirit's grace, is the instrument by means of which Scripture is understood and interpreted. That reason for the Christian is never divorced from the community of faith within which it is formed: 'By experience we all know, that the first outward motive leading men so *to esteem the Scripture* is the authority of God's Church. For when we know the whole Church of God hath that opinion of the Scripture, we judge it even at the first an impudent thing for any man bred and brought up in the Church to be of a contrary mind *without cause.*'[2] Notwithstanding, such authority may not override reason: 'For men to be tied and led by authority, as it were a kind of captivity of judgment ... this were brutish. Again, that authority of men should prevail with men either against or above Reason, is no part of our belief. Companies of learned men be they never so great and reverend, are to yield unto Reason.'[3]

We recall Chadwick's comment that reason in Anglican methodology is neither dogma's submissive handmaid nor unbridled individualism, but a gift of God for the understanding of the faith within the Spirit-led community of faith.

59

For Hooker, human authority is 'the key which openeth the door of entrance into the knowledge of Scripture', but its content is appropriated by the instrumentality of reason. He insists that reason and evidence and 'the authority of men' have all a valid and necessary part to play 'concerning matters of doctrine' – the basic theme of the second book of the *Ecclesiastical Polity*. His thinking is governed by the human search for 'the truth according to the most infallible certainty which the nature of things can yield', and where this is unattainable we incline to the way of 'greatest proba-bility'. No greater reason or probability is 'so sure as that which the Scripture of God teacheth'. Apart from that certainty it is not required that we should assent to anything other 'than such as doth answer the *evidence* which is to be had of that we assent unto'. This applies 'even in matters divine' where we are free to suspend judgment or choose alternatives, and Hooker instances the Fall of men and of angels and the perpetual virginity of Mary. This does not proceed, as some who are perplexed may fear, from lack of faith, because we can be assured that 'such as the evidence is ... such is the heart's assent thereunto'.[4] The same applies to tradition: 'For we do not reject them only because they are not in Scripture, but because they are neither in Scripture, nor can otherwise sufficiently by any reason be proved to be of God.' What can be so proved, 'although unwritten', has the same authority as 'the written laws of God'.[5]

As already noted, Hooker's appeal to Scripture takes account of the different levels of Scripture and this qualifies the way in which the Bible is used, though for him the divine authorship and at least some form of verbal inspiration stand.[6] For example, he distinguishes between what is historically recorded in Scripture and what is binding on the Christian community, a point which has bearing today on the matter of the priestly ordination of women. He criticizes those who readily claim that this or that is against 'God's law' or that 'the word of the Lord' is decisive in a question since:

when they come to allege what word and what law they mean, their common ordinary practice is to quote by-speeches in some *historical* narration or other, and to urge them as if they were written in most exact form of *law* ... . When that which the word of God doth but deliver historically, we construe without any warrant as if it were legally meant, and so urge it further than we can prove that it was intended; do we not add to the laws of God, and make them seem in number more than they are?[7]

Egil Grislis has drawn attention to two further qualifications which Hooker makes to the current view of total inspiration which, together with his affirmation of the instrumental role of reason, ensure that Hooker's appeal to Scripture is never in the form of a literalist biblicism.[8] First of these modifications is his implicit distinction between uninspired and inspired Scripture: 'the belief in the reality of inspiration of some but not all of Scripture allows him to appeal to such revealed truth as is absolutely certain and unquestionable'. This, I would suggest, ties in with the Anglican norm of appeal to the Primitive Church which is always in respect of what Waterland terms 'the prime doctrines'. Hooker's distinction between two levels of Scripture then 'leads him to make use of judicious reasoning in dealing with verses that are not inspired. In this way, his exegetical endeavours are no longer limited to a pedestrian interpretation of Scripture ... but on the grounds of specific exegesis of selected texts and judicious reasoning, he can build a systematic theology that is truly over-arching and encompasses all wisdom available to man.' Hooker indeed looks with reason on Scripture and tradition, and one is reminded of John E. Booty's comment on the Anglican synthesis: 'For Laud, as for Hooker, Scripture contained all things necessary for salvation and was thus supreme. But Scripture presupposes the operation of tradition, reason and church authority, each in its proper place. There is a confluence of God-given instruments and means contributing toward that certainty concerning salvation which is attested by Scripture.'[9]

The second modification discerned by Grislis is 'an expression of basically the same concern [which] may be seen in Hooker's distinction between central and peripheral ideas of Scripture. Here the principle of selectivity is spelled out as Christocentric.' What this means is that any treatment of Scriptural passages which ignores this over-arching design and 'is blind to the overall concerns of Scripture will fail to be a truly faithful interpretation of God's word. In short, while the inspiration of Scripture assures the interpreter that divinely revealed and genuine truth is indeed available, the need for human wisdom and diligent effort is never denied and even explicitly demanded.'

In Hooker we see something perennial, a theological method which is valid today and which declares that a meagre biblicism or an authoritarian traditionalism are foreign to the Anglican ethos. In fact, he said so himself at the close of the second book of the *Polity*:

> Two opinions there are concerning sufficiency of Holy Scripture, each extremely opposite unto the other, *and both repugnant unto truth*. The schools of Rome teach Scripture to be so unsufficient, as if, except traditions were added, it did not contain all revealed and supernatural truth ... others justly condemning this opinion grow likewise unto a dangerous extremity, as if Scripture did not only contain all things in that kind necessary, but all things simply, and in such sort that to do any thing according to any other law were not only unnecessary but even opposite unto salvation, unlawful and sinful.

The bearing of this must be obvious on the contemporary religious scene and also on inter-Church dialogue concerning the nature and role of authority in respect of the Church's articulation of the Faith once for all delivered. How is the 'memory' of the Church authenticated and communicated to the world? What are the tests of that memory and what guarantees the Church's interpretation? Hooker was clear that neither of the extremes is valid, and his warning stands 'lest in attributing unto Scripture more than it can have, the incredibility of that do cause even those things which indeed it hath most abundantly to be less reverently esteemed'.[10]

JEREMY TAYLOR

Hooker's influence went deep in Jeremy Taylor's theology, and by way of confirmation we have the aside of Taylor's friend, George Rust, who averred that 'he would never be governed by anything but reason'. It was central to Taylor's theological synthesis, 'the evidence' (another Hooker echo?) being furnished by Scripture and tradition but 'reason is the judge'.[11] This analysis he sets out in detail in A Discourse of the Liberty of Prophesying (1647), in which he discusses the difficulty of expounding Scripture 'in questions not simply necessary', the uncertainty of tradition in the exposition of Scripture, the fallibility of papal doctrinal determinations, and the disability of the Fathers to determine such non-fundamental questions with certainty. His conclusion is that the authority of reason is in this whole area 'the best judge', and that the duty of faith is complete in the acceptance of the articles of the Apostles' Creed. He distinguishes between the external and the internal means of Scripture exposition, the former being 'church authority, tradition, fathers, councils and decrees of bishops'. The internal means are commentaries, 'conference of places', analogy of reason, analogy of faith. This last is 'but a chimera' if it means any man's faith, and only makes sense if it is 'the rule of faith, that is, the Creed'. Finally, it is suggested that 'consulting the originals is thought a great matter to interpretation of Scriptures' but, says Taylor, the difficulty is in the thing and not in the language – the interpretation is no easier in Greek than in English. These means may be 'good helps' but cannot provide certainty in 'the consideration of the difficulty of Scripture in questions controverted'.[12]

The appeal to Scripture is then to the 'foundation of faith', the Incarnate Word and his teaching, the Risen Lord who is our Life – 'Christ is our medium to God, obedience is the medium to Christ, and faith the medium to obedience.' This faith the Primitive Church held to be fully expressed in the creed, 'a rule of faith to all Christians' as the Fathers explain: 'If this was sufficient to bring men to heaven then, why not now?' This looks like Hooker's different levels of Scripture differently expressed. As Taylor develops this he insists that there is no obligation on Christians to make the articles of faith 'more particular and minute than the creed'. The deductions from these articles 'made more explicit ... by the apostles and others, our fathers in Christ' said no more than what 'lay ... ready formed', and 'the authority of them who compiled the symbol, the plain description of the articles from the words of Scripture, the evidence of reason, demonstrating these to be the whole foundation, are sufficient upon great grounds of reason to ascertain us'. Scripture and reason combine to assure us that 'it is best to rest there, where the apostles and the churches apostolical rested'.

Once more we see the centrality of Scripture and the Primitive Church expounding it in the light of reason. The limits to tradition and to the doctrinal affirmations of the present church are equally clear. The sufficiency for salvation of Scripture and the credal summary of the Gospel does not mean that it is 'unlawful or unsafe for the church ... or any wise man, to extend his own creed to anything which may certainly follow from any one of the articles; but I say that no such deduction is fit to be pressed on others as an article of faith'. He has the whole contemporary religious scene and controversies in view when he concludes: '*The church hath power to intend our faith, but not to extend it; to make our belief more evident, but not more large and comprehensive.*'[13] Taylor develops this later in his book with an awareness of the many difficulties of faith concerning 'the great mysteries' which are in Scripture as well as the clear and plain foundation which is 'set down in Scripture'. He is no mere rationalist, for the element of mystery is central to his sacramental theology and to his conviction that our Christian life is life in Jesus Risen: 'Christ, who is our life'. Nor does reason for Taylor stand alone and solitary: 'Yet reason and human authority are not enemies. For it is a good argument for us to follow such an opinion because it is made sacred by the authority of councils and ecclesiastical tradition, and sometimes it is the best argument we have.'[14] There is always in him an awareness of the human quest for truth and a sense of the balance of the instruments necessary to that process. He believes that in non-foundational doctrinal matters an implicit faith in God is all that is required of the Christian:

> For wherever the word of God is kept, whether in Scripture alone, or also in tradition, he that considers that the meaning of the one, and the truth and certainty of the other, are things of great question, will see a necessity in these things, which are the subject matter of most of the questions of Christendom, that men should hope to be excused by an implicit faith in God Almighty.[15]

This is not the same as having an implicit faith in the Church: 'they who do require an implicit faith in the church, *for articles less necessary* ... do require an implicit faith in the church, because they believe that God hath required of them a mind prepared to believe whatever the church says'. Neither Scripture nor reason give any indication whatever, much less provide any proof, of infallibility attaching to 'any company of men whom we call the church'. The same holds good for papal doctrinal innovations added on to the Rule of Faith of the Primitive Church. Moreover, history provides examples of Popes being adjudged to be in grave error, such as Liberius and Honorius.[16]

Taylor's conclusion is that of a man who looks with reason on the evidence, always admitting the mysterious: 'although we are secured in fundamental points from involuntary error by the plain, express, and dogmatical places of Scripture; yet in other things we are not ... because of the obscurity and difficulty in the controverted parts of Scripture, by reason of the uncertainty of the means of its interpretation, since tradition is of uncertain reputation, and sometimes evidently false'.[17] We are looking at a clear statement concerning the different levels of inspiration in Scripture and an equally clear evaluation of the limits in the appeal to tradition, the essential value of which Taylor never underrates and constantly utilizes in his various writings, bearing in mind at the same time his partial agreement with Daillé. Reason then – and we recall his admiration for Grotius – has a major function in the theological enterprise, but it is not a cold and self-sufficient reason but 'a transcendent that runs through all topics'. It is an exercise of our understanding – 'search the Scriptures' – in what he frequently calls the business of our religion. Moreover, that exercise takes place within the fellowship of faith and with the help of the Holy Spirit: 'right reason, proceeding upon the best grounds it can, viz. of divine revelation and human authority and probability, is our guide, "stando in humanis"; and supposing the assistance of God's Spirit'.[18]

This Spirit of wisdom, he says in his great sermon *Via Intelligentiae*, is also the Spirit of grace who creates 'a new life' in us – we can never forget that Taylor is always the moral/ascetic theologian. The Spirit 'creates a new heart', 'a new principle of life' in us, but 'God's spirit does not destroy reason, but heightens it'. The theme is: 'the way to judge religion is by doing our duty; and theology is rather a divine life than a divine knowledge', following his text, 'If any man will do his will, he shall know the doctrine' (John 7:17). Neither theological systems nor claims to infallibility nor joining in 'phrases of accommodation' will enable us to 'interpret all Scriptures' nor secure us in all truth. Rather, Taylor tells his hearers, must there be a response of the whole person, reason and will and feeling, 'the Spirit of life being the informer of the spirit of man'. Ever present in his theology is the awareness of the Spirit who abides in the Church. We can see clearly in this sermon the influence of his friend Henry More on Taylor's view of reason, which embraces more than the experience of the mind; for 'obedience is the only way to true knowledge', as Rust was to state in Taylor's funeral sermon. The principle is, of course, pure Platonism and its setting forth in this sermon helps to explain a sort of impatience in Taylor with a narrow biblicism and traditionalism and with 'a system or collective body of articles, that tells you, that's the true religion, and they are the church, and the peculiar people of God'.[19]

We are being reminded that reason is the candle of the Lord. There is an open-faced quality in Taylor's thinking and a deep concern that doctrine and life, theology and spirituality, should be in associative harmony. He desires passionately that the Church should be maintained in the truth, the whole truth of obediential faith, by the Spirit's recreative grace and by the Spirit's aid to human reason as it seeks to interpret Scripture, tradition and councils for the here and now and in living continuity with the Church of the Fathers.

Thinking on what Taylor has been saying about the Spirit-filled community and how it authenticates its message, I am irresistibly reminded of what Hans Küng wrote in 1979:

> The conviction of believers from the very beginning was that the Church is maintained quite concretely by God in the truth of Jesus Christ wherever his Spirit, the Holy Spirit of God, is alive and continually bringing fresh guidance into the whole truth; wherever, that is, Jesus himself is and remains the way, the truth, and the life for the individual or for a community; wherever people commit themselves in discipleship to his way; wherever they follow his guidance on their own way of life.[20]

The words might well serve as an introduction to Jeremy Taylor's *The Great Exemplar* (1649), the first life of Christ in English, the fundamental theme of which is that the Life of Christ is continued in the lives of the members of his mystical Body, the Church.

VIII

Scripture and Reason (II)

What we have been attempting to substantiate hitherto is that a hermeneutic of Scripture and tradition is native to Anglicanism, a way of interpreting, a principle of methodology. In other words, it is not enough, as Hooker warns, to claim 'God's law says ...'. You have to ask how you know it is a *law*, and then if it is binding and unchangeable. Or, as Simon Patrick put it, it is not enough to assert 'Tradition lays it down'. You must enquire where the tradition originates and what is the nature of its authority – 'if it be little, its authority is little'.[1] In this process of 'testing the spirits' reason, in Taylor's phrase, is not an enemy to authority but is the Spirit-aided instrument for weighing the evidence and establishing the grounds of authority so that it can stand up to question, as Lambeth 1968 affirmed.

If we look to some other well-known names that figure in various groupings and at various stages of the period, I believe that this will reveal a striking consistency of methodology in this respect. Thus, for example, we find a Latitudinarian like Stillingfleet devoting a book to confirming the thesis of the High Church Laud's *Conference*. There will on occasion be a redistribution of emphasis but the structure of the hermeneutic is basal.

WHICHCOTE AND CULVERWELL

Whichcote's aphorism is saying something that an entire Church was saying: '*The sense of the Church is not a rule; but a thing ruled. The Church is bound unto reason and Scripture, and governed by them as much as any particular person.*' For him, reason is *res illuminata illuminans*, the candle of the Lord, and 'reason is not a shallow thing: it is the first participation from God: therefore he that observes reason, observes God'.[2] It is the concept of reason which we have discerned breaking the surface continually, and we meet the same picture of reason as a derivative light in the discourses of his fellow Cambridge Platonist, Nathanael Culverwell: 'Surely there's none can think that light is primitively and originally in the candle; but they must look upon that only as a weak participation of something that is more bright and glorious.'[3]

As with Whichcote there is no 'irreconcilable jarring' for him between faith and reason. There is a 'twin-light' from both because they 'spring from the same fountain of light'. By ignoring this the followers of Socinus 'made shipwrack of the faith', allowing everything to the 'meer pretences of reason [but] because Socinus has burnt his wings at this candle of the Lord, must none other use it?' Reason without revelation is quite inadequate and incomplete for 'faith is a supply of reason in things intelligible, as the imagination is of light in things visible'. In a lovely phrase he says, 'You may see Socrates in the twilight ... telling you that his lamp will shew him nothing but his own darkness.' He writes with a fluid style and attractive imagery, and if Whichcote could say, 'A man's reason is no where so much satisfied as in matters of faith', Culverwell puts it more strikingly: 'The light of reason doth no more prejudice the light of faith, than the light of a candle doth extinguish the light of a star.'[4] He was part of the Cambridge Platonists' dual effort 'to vindicate the use of reason in matters of religion ... and ... on the other hand to chastise the sawciness of Socinus and his followers, who dare set Hagar above her mistress, and make faith unite at the elbow of corrupt and distorted reason'.[5] So wrote his friend and contemporary editor, revealing the deep currents of dogmatism and of emerging liberality which were running counter in religion then, and which still run. As theologians, the Cambridge Platonists were simultaneously fighting on two fronts, resisting the extremes of Calvinism in 'the decrees' and promoting reason as an essential element in religious thought and doctrinal formulations.

Not surprisingly then, like Hooker, he puts reason before tradition in order of importance: 'As for all other sacred antiquity, though I shall ever honour it ... yet if antiquity shall stand in competition with this Lamp of the Lord ... it must not think much if we prefer reason, a daughter of eternity, before antiquity which is the offspring of time.' However, the divine authorship of the Scriptures and the uniqueness of their content set them quite apart. They are foundational, but not so with tradition: 'Of the two *the Church hath more security in resting upon genuine reason* than in relying upon some spurious traditions; for think but a while upon those infinite deceits and uncertainties that such historical conveyances are liable and exposed to, I always except those sacred and heavenly volumes of Scripture, that are strung together as so many pearls.' 'Their certainty' is borrowed not from universal tradition but from 'those points of divinity in them'.[6]

MORE AND HALES

Henry More, whose influence on the thinking of his friend Jeremy Taylor is clearly discernible, was, by reason of the variety of his interests, at once the most typical and the most intriguing of this distinguished group. Primarily a theologian, he was as an early member of the Royal Society actively interested in the new science and deeply immersed in mystical and vitalistic speculation. Plotinus and Ficino gave to More and his colleagues a filtered Platonism. He does not have the easily flowing style of Culverwell or the at times curious modernity of Smith, but there is in his voluminous and wide-ranging works a pervasive serenity and a sense of harmony. Yet in spite of his strongly mystical bent More could write, 'I conceive Christian religion rational throughout', and: 'To take away reason ... is to rob Christianity of that special prerogative it has above all other religions in the world, namely, that it dares appeal unto reason.' For him, reason comes not only from ratiocination but from 'a certain principle more noble and inward than reason itself. ... I have a sense of something in me ... which I must confess is of so retruse a nature that I want a name for it, unless I should adventure to term it Divine Sagacity, which is the first rise of successful reason.'

More's spiritual depth leads him to see reason as coming from the 'integrity of the will and affections' and keeping company with holiness, 'a pure and unspotted mind', because what he calls 'intellectual sense' is 'from the presence of God ... who endues the mind with that Divine Sagacity, which is more inward ... ever antecedaneous to that reason which in theories of greatest importance approves itself afterwards'.[7] Ultimately, as for Taylor, the goal is obediential faith. In his *Explanation of the Grand Mystery of Godliness* (1660), he insists that the indispensable duty is the conformity of the Christian life, the root of which is obediential faith. Its parts are charity, humility, and purity, justice, temperance, fortitude and prudence.[8] There is an everyday quality of practical realism merged with a sense of mystery, a concern with the mystical aspect of things.

If a mysticism of reason is not a contradiction in terms then we catch something of it in More and recognize that here is a deeply Christian intellectual grappling with the problems of a transitional period. In *The Antidote against Atheism* (1652) he maintains that the alternative to atheism is not 'blinde obedience to the Authority of a Church' but the use of reason in religion.[9] A similar line is followed in his *Brief Discourse of Enthusiasm* (1662). Enthusiasm is based on 'the magisterial dictates of an over-bearing fancy' which rejects reason's 'deliberate examination'. Enthusiasm is 'a misconceit of being inspired'.[10] In the dedication to Cudworth of his *Conjectura Cabbalistica* (1662) he sets out his basic approach which 'will neither antiquate Truth for the oldness of the notion, nor slight her for looking young, or bearing the face of novelty'. Only an enthusiast can 'exclude reason in the search of Divine truth'. There is in this work a blend of mysticism and reason, as when he writes: 'how much the more the inward and mysterious meaning of the Text makes for reverence of the Holy Scripture ... whereas the urging of the bare literal sense has either made or confirmed many an atheist'.

Interestingly for our present theme, More, in his *Preface*, speaks of a triple interpretation of the three first chapters of Genesis, a literal, a philosophical and a mystical interpretation: 'Yet I call the whole interpretation but a conjecture.' This throws an unexpected light on the handling of the Biblical text at this time. He returns again to the subject in *A Modest Enquiry* (1664), Part II, where he is referring to the creation-story as adapted to its listeners: 'But though a man be himself sufficiently persuaded of the historical truth of the symbols, yet I question whether he be over-confidently to avow the certainty thereof in every passage to men of a more philosophical genius. And the rather, because very sober and well-approved writers have affirmed some of them parabolical.' Having named these authors, More concludes that a literalist view is shaky: 'Wherefore it were very indiscreet, whereas both some Christians of the better note, as also Philo and other Jews, make several passages of these chapters parabolical, to avow to a philosopher that they are all of them really historical, whatever a man may conceive in his own breast touching this matter.' When we remember that More's 'philosopher' is a scientist, we recall that part of his mission is to make it reasonable for a scientist to believe. He professes deep loyalty to the Church of England, to its Orders and Sacraments, and in the *Explanation of the Grand Mystery of Godliness* (1660) he says of the Restoration that it means 'the recovery of the Church to her ancient apostolick purity'. All non-essentials may no longer be treated as binding, but only *'that doctrine that depends not upon the fallible deductions of men, but is plainly set down in the Scripture; other things being left at the free recommendation of the Church'*.[11]

This is the classical Anglican stance and More proceeds to apply it to the contemporary religious scene and to the authentication of doctrine. Typically of this position which we have been evaluating, his overall design in a book which is 'a sort of *summa* of the Christian religion, based on the Gospels',[12] is to demonstrate 'the solidity of the fundamentals'.[13] For More the appeal to tradition is strictly limited by the appeal to Scripture and by the appeal to reason.

What I am trying to show is how he handled both these controls and how they functioned in his understanding of religion with its central concept of the Divine life, 'the root of which is an obediential faith and affiance in the true God'.[14] For him, religious experience cannot be severed from the historical content of the New Testament which validates it. His appeal to Scripture is both to its historical objectivity and to the life-changing impact of what is there factually related – these are not just two aspects but an inseparable impress: 'For whereas some in an hypocritical flattery of the external Person of Christ shuffle out all obligation to the Divine Life, that mystical Christ within us, and pervert the grace of God ... I have with undeniable clearness of testimony *from Reason and Scripture* demonstrated the truth and necessity of both Christ within and Christ without.'[15] Two years later he would return to the subject in the Preface to *The Immortality of the Soul* (1662), noting that some 'have become ... misbelievers of the whole history of Christ, and ... look upon the mystery of Christianity as a thing wholly within us, and that has no other object than what is either acting or acted in ourselves'. Equally mistaken is the over-concentration on the objective and historical aspect, which minimizes 'all obligation to the divine life, that mystical Christ within us'. In other words, theology and spirituality, the historical and the experiential, cannot be sundered without destroying religion; and he observes the proof of this in some of the extreme sects arising during the Commonwealth period. While he fairly criticizes doctrinal positions, such as 'the opinions of solafidianism and Eternal Decrees', which appear to him to be unscriptural and unreasonable, More shares that tolerance of others charac-teristic of the Platonists: 'a mutual agreement of bearing with one another's *dissents in the non-fundamentals* of religion is really a greater ornament of Christianity than the most exact uniformity imaginable, it being an eminent act or exercise of charity'.[16]

The permissible or legitimate area of divergence, how-ever, is outside the fundamentals, and this says something

significant concerning the nature of the control which
Scripture exercises – 'the solidity of the fundamentals'. While
he holds that episcopacy is 'recommended to us both from
the practice of the Primitive Church and the light of Reason
... I should sooner venture upon Mr Thorndike's way than
any ... it being such a mixture of Episcopacy and Presbytery
together as may justly ... satisfy the expectations of both
parties'.[17] He is firmly opposed to 'overmuch idolized
doctrines' such as imputative righteousness or that 'a bare
faith will justify us', on the grounds that they are not '*consonant with Reason, nor the rest of Scripture*'.[18] Quite simply,
More is demonstrating the intelligent appeal to Scripture,
that is, to Scripture and reason, which it is the purpose of
this chapter to establish as an essential in the spirit of
Anglicanism.

The universality of this outlook in seventeenth-century
Anglicanism and the unsuitability, indeed the impossibility,
of categorizing by 'parties' is vividly illustrated by John
Hales, 'the Ever Memorable'. A leading figure in the new
historical and critical theology of the Tew Circle, he was
appointed chaplain by the High Church Archbishop Laud,
who was godfather to the best known of the group, William
Chillingworth. Hales shared the tolerant outlook of the
Cambridge Platonists and, like Henry More, declined all
preferment: 'Let it not offend any that I have made
Christianity rather an Inn to receive all than a private house
to receive some few.'[19] Scripture and reason are inseparable
companions in religion, the core of which he understands
to be faith working through love in obedience to the
commandments.[20] In sharp contrast with the sectaries of his
day Hales writes that 'the sense is Scripture rather than the
words'. Those who handle the Biblical text 'as chemists deal
with natural bodies, torturing them to extract out of
them that which God and nature never put in them' are
engaged in a futile exercise because Scripture interprets the
interpreter.[21] Profoundly convinced of the vital role of reason
in religion he makes no idol of it, commenting that 'the too
great presumption upon the strength and subtlety of our

own wits' can lead us to abuse Scripture.[22] On the contrary, the Holy Spirit works within the community of faith: 'When the Spirit regenerates a man, it infuses no knowledge of any point of faith, but sends him to the Church, and to the Scriptures.'[23]

What is central is that the only ground of faith is what is plain in Scripture, the essentials of the Gospel: 'For it is not depth of knowledge, nor knowledge of antiquity, nor sharpness of wit, nor authority of councils, nor the name of the Church, that can settle the restless conceits that possess the minds of many doubtful Christians.'[24] It is true that there are apparent contradictions and that there are non-essentials, but concerning these 'it shall well befit our Christian modesty to participate somewhat of the sceptic'.[25] The distinction of fundamentals from secondary truths, such as the various views about predestination, must be preserved: 'that which keeps the Churches this day so far asunder [is] this peremptory manner of setting down our conclusions, under this high commanding form of necessary truths'.[26] In such matters, reason is the best guide 'where Scripture is ambiguous',[27] and always the plain sense of Scripture is to be followed. If then 'the words admit a double sense, and I follow one, who can assure me that that which I follow is the truth? For infallibility in judgment or interpretation, or whatsoever, is annexed neither to the See of any Bishop, nor to the Fathers, nor to the Councils, nor to the Church, nor to any created power whatsoever.'[28] As for interpreting Scripture 'by allegorising or allusion', favoured by 'a great part of antiquity', this may have its place but for the literal interpretation he favours 'the interpreters of our own times, because of their skill in the Original languages, *their care of pressing the circumstances and coherence of the text, of comparing like places of Scripture with like*'.[29] Nevertheless, he adds, 'I speak not to discountenance antiquity, but that all ages ... may have their due.' Thus, Hales gives us an insight into the way in which the Biblical text was being handled by a devout scholar, generous and constructive, for whom reason has an essential function in religion but who recommends more 'maybes and peradventures', more 'old men's modesty'.[30]

There comes to mind once again not a vague liberalism but Alec Vidler's liberality, the opposite not of conservatism but of intransigence, a quality flexible and vital.[31] It is a word without the controversial party-associations of 'liberalism' and it draws its strength from scripturalness, historicity and rationality. It is of the essence of the Anglican way and to loosen our hold on it is to imperil a heritage. Charles Gore saw this with clarity in the nineteen-thirties. Elsewhere I wrote of the continuity of this approach with that of the *Lux Mundi* (1889) essayists, and in particular with Gore:

> For both groups shared an outlook, and to some extent limitations, but they were determined to face the issues raised by contemporary knowledge, being equally convinced that what was needed was not *concession* in regard to fundamentals, but *restatement*, and refusal to add to them. This synthesis was primarily effected for Gore through the medium of his concept of authority which was framed in terms of reason. Throughout his development of his theory of authority, the real thread of continuity is confidence in reason. Gore himself wrote that Anglicanism does not acquiesce in the severance of reason and authority (one remembers Jeremy Taylor and Henry Chadwick on this) and he gave firm adherence to the threefold combination of Scripture, tradition and reason.

Gore considered it the advantage and attraction of Anglicanism to have retained hold on the 'ancient structure of the Church', while at the same time welcoming 'the new learning, *the new appeal to Scripture*, the freedom of historical criticism and the duty of private judgment'. He set great store by the appeal to Scripture, stressing the value of antiquity, and he gave it as his opinion that 'it is this appeal ... which qualifies the Catholicism of the Church of England as scriptural and liberal'. It is worth noting too (as do James Carpenter and Michael Ramsey[32]) that Gore's phrase 'liberal Catholicism' drew its essential meaning from these pervading ideas of scripturalness, historicity and rationality, so that when using it he was in fact describing the historic position of Anglicanism and he did not have theological liberalism in mind at all.[33] This is to be borne in mind as Anglicans assess and evaluate the principles by means of which faith and practice are authenticated. The primary basis of authority is Scripture. Reason is interpretative and functions now, as it did in the first centuries, within the living Church which is at once the guardian and the subject of the Scripture in and through the Spirit who abides in the Church, leading us into the truth that is ever old and ever new.

HENRY HAMMOND (1605–1660):
'The father of English Biblical criticism'

Hammond, with his tremendous literary output and extensive and exact scholarship, was a central figure in the Laudian group during the Commonwealth. Not only did his work provide an intellectual defence for the dispossessed Church, but he encouraged others to write and he organized support for the Anglican cause. His books, including his *Practical Catechism* (1646), *Of Schisme: A Defence of the Church of England* (1653), and his six shorter works on practical aspects of moral theology,[34] constituted a major single contribution to the maintenance and restoration of Anglican confidence when outwardly all seemed to be lost. We have already taken note of his respect for tradition in its supportive and interpretative function; and Hammond's *Dissertationes Quatuor* (1651), in which he refuted Salmasius and Blondel and affirmed episcopacy from the Ignatian epistles, established as genuine by Ussher and Voss, proved to be a significant support to Anglicans striving to uphold their identity in a time of flux. He assesses the Scriptural evidence for ecclesiastical polity from the New Testament and then evaluates the evidence from patristic sources, 'the best records of Primitive Antiquity'. This is how he uses the appeal to tradition. It is, however, with his handling of Scripture that we are immediately concerned, and in this basic area of theology Hammond's ranking is high.

In his authoritative study, John William Packer writes: 'In the field of biblical criticism Henry Hammond was one of the first English scholars to compare the manuscripts of the New Testament, and to examine the language in which it was written to discover its most exact meaning. He also considered the background of the New Testament to find out what light it could throw on the interpretation of the text', and he quotes G. G. Perry that 'It is not too much to say that Dr Hammond is the father of English Biblical criticism'.[35] It is a view confirmed by R. L. Colie, with the interesting implication, which we have already suggested, that this methodology was common to Platonist, Arminian and Latitudinarian alike: 'Henry Hammond, whose annotations upon the Bible were to stand for his Church in the place of the Genevan annotations, still influential in England, was strongly Arminian.'[36] The chief of these works by Hammond was *A Paraphrase and Annotations upon all the Books of the New Testament, briefly explaining all the difficult places thereof.* This appeared in 1650, followed by *A Paraphrase and Annotations upon the Book of the Psalms* (1659), and his *A Paraphrase on the ten first Chapters of the Proverbs* was posthumously published in 1683.

What was special about these books and in what way do they bear on our present theme? The special quality in Hammond's works is his approach to the Biblical text, anticipating future developments: 'The understanding the word of God contain'd in the Scripture, is no work of extraordinary illumination, but must be attained by the same means, or the like, by which other writings of men are expounded, and no otherwise.' This is from his *A Postscript concerning New Light or Divine Illumination* in which he rejects the New Light propounded by the sects:

> that the understanding or interpreting the word of God ... is not imputable to the use of ordinary means such as are the assistance of God's Spirit joyned with the use of learning, study, meditation, rational inference ... consulting of the original languages, and ancient copies, and expositions of Fathers of the Church ... but either to the extraordinary gift of the Spirit in prophesying, preaching and expounding.

He insists that only a sound and conservative doctrine of Scripture will serve, and in the Advertisement to the Reader in the *Paraphrase and Annotations upon all the Books of the New Testament* (1653) he notes that he generally contents himself 'with the one primary and literal sense of each place' except where there is 'just reason of doubting betwixt two or more senses'.

The bearing of this on our theme of Scripture and reason is then obvious. Hammond has a hermeneutic of Scripture by means of which human reason assisted by the Spirit illumines and interprets the written Word. He is part of the movement of the Church, struggling under oppression and sequestration, to formulate a theology and a spirituality which would be able to cope with the demands of the changing society and the new scientific outlook then emerging.

This is underlined by his admiration for his friend Hugo Grotius whom he supported in three different books, the best known being his *A Second Defence of the Learned Hugo Grotius* (1655). The Dutch theologian, an admirer of Anglicanism, had published his *Annotationes* on the Old and New Testaments in 1642 and Hammond paid tribute to him and followed his method of exegesis: 'This introduced a close study of the text into biblical criticism and discarded the belief in literal inspiration. He did *not disregard the importance of ecclesiastical tradition* in the right understanding of the scriptures but he saw it as *subsidiary* to a detailed interpretation of the original text itself.' [37] The way in which this ties in with the subject of the limits in the appeal to tradition is evident, and Packer cites a letter from Hammond implying Grotius's approval that 'the Church of England's Cause will never suffer at that Tribunal of the primitive Church or Apostolic Tradition, sufficiently testified to be such'. In the same letter he describes the Dutch scholar as 'a great lover of the Church of England, wherein he had an ambition to have liv'd and dyed'.[38]

The title of Hammond's *Of the Reasonableness of Christian Religion* (1650) indicates a quality endemic to

Anglicanism, as witness similar books with similar titles during the period. There come to mind, for example, Stillingfleet's *Rational Account of the Christian Faith* (1662), Baxter's *The Reasons of the Christian Religion* (1666), and Ussher's *Principles of Christian Religion* (1654). Having discussed Scriptural and patristic evidence, Hammond claims that the validity of the testimony on which Christian faith is founded 'will render the belief rational'.[39] What is striking is the similarity in certain respects with the treatment of Latitudinarians such as Wilkins and Tillotson, once more underscoring the unity of theological method. We have seen how he also has a hermeneutic of tradition in his *Of Fundamentals*, where he concludes that the Creed, delivered by the Primitive Church and 'expounded in the homilies of the Fathers ... is in all reason to be deemed the sum of that foundation'.[40] His work demonstrates a balanced theological method by which, building on a clear-cut understanding as to what may legitimately be regarded as constituting fundamentals, Scripture and tradition are held in a creative relationship with reason.

What we are looking at then in the course of this survey is a religion not of biblicism or of traditionalism but one in which, to quote Paul Avis, 'it was owing to the balancing factors of reason, conscience and the Hookerian sense of what is appropriate to the circumstances, that tradition and antiquity were not permitted to become sources of authority, but were confined to the ancillary role of general guidance and sources of relevant evidence in doctrinal debate'.[41] It is a religion not of diktats but of consensus, in which the centrality of Scripture and the visible continuity of the Church, both confirmed by antiquity, are held as one and illuminated in each successive age by the freedom of reason to interpret Scripture and assess tradition. It is a religion which regards reason as the gift of the Spirit for the interpretation and application of the Faith once for all delivered, not as omnicompetent but as hermeneutical.

STILLINGFLEET AND OTHERS

The Latitudinarians have been accused of ignoring tradition but this is far from being the case, as may be seen in the work of Edward Stillingfleet (1635–99) one of the most prominent of the group. He set great store by 'the judgment of antiquity ... especially of the three first centuries; and the reasons for it', and he held that the Fathers' defence of the Christian religion is 'manifested to concur fully with our way of resolving faith'. What is true is that, like Hooker and Taylor, he placed tradition last in the threefold appeal: 'And *next to Scripture and Reason*, I attribute so much to the sense of the Christian Church in the ages *next succeeding the Apostles*, that it is no mean confirmation to me of the truth of the Protestant way of resolving faith ... so exactly concurring ... to the unanimous consent of antiquity.'[42]

So, what was that way? Stillingfleet goes straight to Scripture and reason by way of discussing what he terms 'resolving faith': 'when we speak of the resolution of faith, by faith we understand a rational and discursive act of the mind. For faith being an assent upon evidence, or reason inducing the mind to assent, it must be a rational act'. He is not speaking of faith as 'an infused habit of grace'. That the Spirit operates so that 'saving faith is wrought in us' is true but 'comes not home to the question', which is about the grounds of Christian religion and why we assent to them. There are, therefore, 'three questions to be resolved. First, Why I believe those things to be true which are contained in the Book called the Scripture? 2. Why I believe the doctrine contained in that Book to be divine? 3. Why I believe the Books themselves to be of Divine Revelation?'[43]

This is going to the root of the matter and the objective is to show that the Church of England's way of establishing the certainty of 'the grounds of faith ... is satisfactory and reasonable'. There is all the difference in the world, he suggests in the Epistle Dedicatory, between the faith that moves mountains and the faith that swallows mountains. We pause to recall that the book is a confirmation of Laud's

Conference, its method and conclusions concerning the exposition of the Church's faith by Anglicans. We do so noting that Stillingfleet's title is *A Rational Account*; and while his methodology is on all fours with that of the earlier work the emphasis is changed, or rather redistributed, so that while 'Scripture, reason, or the consent of the Primitive Church'[44] remain the standard of assay, reason is hermeneutical. He outlines his approach:

> There remains nothing then but Reason ... by which I must prove, that the Scriptures are from God, which Reason partly makes use of the Church's Tradition not in any notion of infallibility, but merely as built on principles common to human nature, and partly uses those other arguments which prove by the greatest rational evidence, that the doctrine contained in Scripture, was from God.[45]

There is a Hookerian echo in 'But still as the assent is, so the evidence must be'.[46] Stillingfleet claims that the way of deciding questions by infallibility 'destroys all rational evidence of the truth of religion';[47] and the emphasis on evidence, seen in Hooker and Taylor, is heavier and reflects the changed world of Stillingfleet in which science and a questioning modernity had made their appearance.

However, he is far from ignoring the appeal to antiquity or its value, as we have seen. It is simply that history shows the Fathers to have relied on Scripture and reason to commend the Faith to their times. He instances Clement of Alexandria: 'Thus we see that he insists on rational evidence as the great and sufficient testimony into which our Faith is resolved as to the being of a Divine Revelation.'[48] For the Primitive Church presented the faith in Scripture and claimed the support of reason to commend it: 'What was it then, I pray, that Justin Martyr, of a philosopher becoming a Christian, resolved his Faith into? If we may believe himself, it was into the evidence of the Doctrine of Christianity, and not into the infallibility of any Church.' Stillingfleet draws the same conclusions from Irenaeus: 'Although Irenaeus of all the ancient Fathers be looked on as the most favourable to tradition ... yet I doubt not but to make it appear, that where he speaks most concerning tradition, he makes the resolution to be wholly and intirely to the Scripture.' In other words, Stillingfleet, who takes a favourable view of the appeal to tradition, is making it clear that it is *limited by Scripture and reason*. He takes the same line on oral traditions and on the identification of the teaching of 'the present church' as being the Tradition. He says of Irenaeus, by way of comment on the first subject:

> his appeal to tradition was only in a matter of fact, whether ever any such thing as their opinion [i.e. the Valentinians] which was not contained in Scripture, was delivered to them by the Apostles or no i.e. Whether the Apostles left any oral traditions in the Churches which should be the rule to inter- pret Scriptures by, or no? And the whole design of Irenaeus is to prove the contrary.[49]

Stillingfleet is caustic on the subject of appealing to antiquity to authenticate doctrinal innovations in order to justify 'the sentence of the present Church' as definitive: 'So long as they think they can make them serve their turns, then, Who but the Fathers? If they appear refractory, and will not serve as hewers of wood and drawers of water to them, then, Who are the Fathers? It is the Church's judgment they rely on, and not the Fathers.'[50] Finally, the role of Scripture is primary in any assessment of tradition: 'Nothing ought to be looked on as an article of faith among the Fathers but what they declare that they believe in account of Divine revela- tion.' Neither is there any probative value in the opinion of a couple of Fathers unless 'all who had occasion to mention it, did speak of it as the doctrine of the Church'. Similarly, a tradition has no force if it is built 'upon the sense of doubtful places in Scripture … in this case, the enquiry is taken off from the judgment of the Fathers, and fixed upon the sense of Scriptures which they and we both rely upon'.[51] In other words, Scripture authenticates and reason interprets and 'the judgment of the first three centuries' is valuable as corroborative.

Stillingfleet was a significant figure in the Church and in his *Origines Sacrae: A Rational Account of the Grounds of the Christian Faith as to the Truth and Divine Authority of the Scriptures* (1662) he made a valiant, if only partially successful, attempt to demonstrate that the new movements of thought and the developing science were not detrimental to religion and to the Bible as a valid source of authority. Boyle the scientist, Ray the naturalist, Hobbes and Descartes feature in a work which shows a theologian coming to grips with hitherto unprecedented questions, and remaining convinced that while 'that is not revealed which is not made intelligible ... the immediate dictates of natural light are no sufficient standard to judge of Divine revelation by'.[52]

Apart from Stillingfleet and Gilbert Burnet the Latitudinarians produced few books, but their influence was widespread, the most notable example being John Tillotson who became Archbishop of Canterbury in 1691. He was primarily a preacher and Burnet wrote of him that 'the nation proposed him as a pattern'. The practical thrust of his sermons is to set out 'the whole duty of man' and their doctrinal aim is to show that 'speculative atheism is unreasonable'.[53] As to Christian believing and behaving, an obedient man has not 'the least ground to suspect any latent or secret decree of God against him to work his ruin'.[54] Just as he rejects a theology of 'the decrees' so he refuses a theology of assurance, 'that the Gospel is all promises and our part is onely ... to be confident that God will perform them if we can but think so, though we do nothing else'.[55] Our vocation is to duty by grace and this is the Anglican way, 'sober' and 'reasonable', and he considers 'the Church of England to be the best constituted Church this day in the world'.[56]

His parochial sermons for the chief festivals are direct and forceful, stressing the Scriptural nature of Anglican teaching. On a number of occasions Tillotson makes use of the support afforded by the writings of the Fathers, but his central theme is that Christianity is 'the best and most reasonable religion in the world'.[57] Twice he insists that *'reason is the faculty whereby revelation is to be discerned'* [58] and 'it does not alter the case much to give reason ill names'.[59] The characteristic

Latitudinarian emphasis on reason is everywhere in sermons which strive to be Scriptural and devotionally practical – 'We may not think that we are justified by faith as it is separate from hope and charity.' [60] For Tillotson, reason is not simply hermeneutical for Scripture and tradition but an essential element in the presentation of Christian faith: 'I know not how it comes to pass, but so it is, that everyone that offers to give a reasonable account of his Faith, and to establish religion upon rational principles, is presently branded for a Socinian.' [61] In the same sermon he can imagine no greater disservice to religion that 'bearing the world in hand, that men ought to believe without reason, for this is to turn faith into credulity'.

Thomas Tenison, who succeeded Tillotson as Archbishop of Canterbury, gives a balanced picture of the Anglican use of Scripture and reason in the determining of doctrinal questions, and one in which the appeal to tradition is not marginalized but circumscribed. In *The Difference betwixt the Protestant and Socinian Methods* (1687) we note his use of the term 'method', or as we might put it, 'methodology', and the fact that Scripture is above reason, allowing for the category of mystery in religion. This is unusual in one of his school.

> We have a greater veneration for the Holy Scripture itself, than the right Socinian: For such a one *makes reason the rule of that rule*; and though he thinks a doctrine is plain in Scripture, yet, if he believes it to be against his reason, he assents not to it. Whereas a man of this Church believes the Scriptures to be written by inspiration of God: And, upon that account he assures himself that nothing contrary to true reason can be contained in the Scriptures. Therefore when he finds anything in Holy Writ which to him is incomprehensible, he does not say he believes it though it be impossible and irrational; *but he believes it to be rational though mysterious*; and he suspects not reason itself, but his own present art of reasoning whensoever it concludes against that which he reads and reads without doubting of the sense of the words: and *by meditation* he at last finds his error. [62]

This is interesting because Tenison is making it clear that he does not regard reason as omnicompetent and that the appeal to reason is also limited by the intrinsic authority of Scripture itself and by the possibility of a flaw in an individual's process of reasoning. In the same way, he sets out the value and the limits of the appeal to tradition:

> 'Though the modern Arians and Socinians do speak of Tradition, and not of Scripture only, yet our plea and their's is not perfectly the same. Touching the Holy Scripture, we have a greater veneration for it then many of them: and for Tradition, though we make it not the very Rule of our Faith, nor place infallibility in it; yet, in concurrence with Scripture, it weigheth not so much with them as with us.[63]

This is the stance with which we have become familiar, and Tenison goes on to make the point stressed by his predecessors, that 'We do not under-value the Fathers, but proceed in the method of the Antients who began first with the Holy Scripture, and then descended to those who wrote next after the Holy Penmen.'[64] It is relevant to record that the design of his book is to demonstrate the appeal to Scripture, Tradition and Reason as the Anglican 'method' in the authentication of doctrine.

It is the method which, with variations of emphasis, governs the thinking on doctrinal determinations in the wide range of theologians, formularies and formulations which we have been evaluating. Nor was it confined to those whose profession was theology: its influence was so pervasive that it was for an intelligent layman like Sir Thomas Browne the natural way of thinking about religion, about decision-making in disputed areas and about the commitment of the Christian to the Church. Early in the book which charmed successive generations, his *Religio Medici* (1642/3), he records that while as a Christian 'I meerely owe this title to the Font' his later experience of life and his 'confirmed judgement' led him so that 'I finde my self obliged by the principles of grace and the law of mine owne reason, to embrace no other name but this'. His commitment to the Church of England is total:

There is no Church whose every part so squares unto my conscience, whose articles, constitutions, and customes seeme so consonant unto reason, and as it were framed to my particular devotion, as this whereof I hold my beliefe, the Church of England, to whose faith I am a sworne subject, and therefore in a double obligation, subscribe unto her Articles, and endeavour to observe her Constitutions: whatsoever is beyond, as points indifferent, I observe according to the rules of my private reason, or the humor and fashion of my devotion ... In briefe, where the Scripture is silent, the Church is my Text; where that speaks, 'tis but my Comment; where there is a joynt silence of both, I borrow not the rules of my Religion from Rome or Geneva, but the dictates of my owne reason.[65]

Browne is as robustly Anglican as he is loving and non-judgmental to his fellow-Christians of other traditions. His moving *confessio fidei* will most fittingly round off our investigation. That investigation has not been an antiquarian exercise or a merely historical survey. Rather does it uncover a perennial quality in the communicating of the transcendent Gospel by Anglicans to different ages, social situations and particular cultures. It is a dynamic approach to the presentation of the faith once for all delivered, living and effective today, as one can see from the section-report on dogmatic and pastoral concerns of the last Lambeth Conference (1988): 'The Church itself is a community of interpretation, understanding and applying the mind of Christ using reliable sources and reliable agencies. This involves the co-ordinated use of Scripture, tradition and reason, guided by office holders, prophets and sages and the whole body of believers.'[66]

IX

A Summation and Lambeth 1988

The same Lambeth 1988 document witnesses throughout to this continuing method in Anglicanism and firmly sites the discussion in the present:

> Tradition and reason, then, are two distinct contexts in which the Scriptures speak and out of which they are interpreted. It is in the interplay and the conflict between them – between the common mind of the Church and the common mind of a culture – that the meaning of the Gospel for a particular time and place is to be discerned. Indeed it could be argued that tradition – what we have called the 'mind' of the Church – is the repository of just such discernments stimulated by the tradition and the language of a particular culture. To be involved in this dialogical situation is always uncomfortable. It becomes dangerous, perhaps, only when what is properly a dialogue becomes a monologue delivered at length by only one of its parties. Tradition and reason need each other if God's Word is to be shared.[1]

The way in which this is confirmatory of our researches into the outworking of the Anglican ethos hardly needs stressing. The document clearly echoes in the present the Anglican consensus from the past. What we have been looking at hitherto is an evaluation of tradition and its role in the authenticating of the faith and practice through which the Church preaches the Gospel and its implications for the community-life of God's people and for God's world. It is an evaluation of tradition which is both appreciative and critical, always taking full account of its force but firmly circumscribing the range of its authority within the threefold partnership. The appeal to tradition has invariably been made in this context of the appeal to Scripture and to reason.

Tradition is embodied in a world of process but its movement and the outcome of the process are controlled by Scripture and interpreted by reason, itself a constituent in the authentication and verification of doctrine and praxis.

Anglicans have consistently seen tradition as corroborative and interpretative of Scripture and as having different levels. This has always been linked in with the appeal to the Primitive Church as to 'the prime antiquity of the Church' (Taylor), the first level of tradition which is nevertheless still 'a subordinate rule' (White). The central Anglican use of tradition is then, as Laud put it, 'Scripture and the primitive Church expounding it'. The Primitive Church is a 'standard' (Wake), and this is the primary level of tradition, its chief function being doctrinal corroboration and the exclusion of doctrinal innovations added on to the faith once for all delivered; 'but the Tradition of all ages is one thing and the Authority of the present Church is another' (Chillingworth). The present Church has authority to make changes as occasion demands in matters of polity, but 'the matter of faith is constant' (Hooker). Like the Primitive Church the present Church is controlled in its interpretation of the Faith by the Scriptures, and the appeal to the Early Church is invariably in respect of 'prime doctrines', the *hapax*. Inseparably part of the *hapax*/tradition relationship is the distinction between fundamentals of doctrine and worship and secondary matters, and this is an essential element in the operation of the threefold appeal in doctrinal authentication.

Behind and through all is the unceasing work of the Spirit, guiding the mind of the Church as it interprets the Gospel and illuminating human reason, which is God's gift for the understanding of the faith, an instrument through which the elements of authority are kept in proportion. Reason is thus an essential part of the response of the whole person and of the community of faith to that Gospel, through the Spirit of grace. Tradition in this sense is then the continuing response of the Church as it receives and interprets the Word of God, as a judge interprets and expounds the law to which he himself is subject. Just as the subordination of the appeal to tradition to the primary element, the appeal to Scripture, is a constant, so is the difference between traditionalism and the intelligent appeal to tradition a permanent feature in the Anglican presentation of the Faith. If the material we have been reviewing demonstrates one thing more than another, it is that the appeal to reason is deeply embedded in the Anglican psyche. The whole thrust of the unceasing explicit emphasis on the threefold appeal has been and is to prevent the monologue referred to in the Lambeth 1988 section-report on dogmatic and pastoral concerns.

We have taken note of how the Lambeth Conferences of 1948 and 1968 handled the subject of Christian authority and the role of tradition within the exercise of that authority which stems from the risen Christ whose Life continues in the lives of the members of his mystical Body, the Church. Because the Spirit of truth and grace abides in the Church, 'the continuing experience of the Holy Spirit through his faithful people in the Church' (Lambeth 1948), the *consensus fidelium*, is an element in this authority. Or, as Lambeth 1988 puts it, 'there is an essential authority that belongs to the body of believers as a whole … in the end doctrine, however proposed or defined, must be *received* by the body of believers to whom it is addressed as consonant with Scripture and tradition'.[2] This modern document in its analysis tallies in general terms with the results of our examination of the Anglican tradition from Jewel onwards, throwing fresh light on the questions we have been considering and transposing them into our contemporary context. Like the classical Anglican authors, the Lambeth section-report on authority is deeply aware of the Spirit abiding in the Church. Authority's function is to transmit a way of life deriving from Christ Risen and conferred by the Father through the Spirit's working, enabling the members to enter this Life and to live it out. The Life is conveyed by the Spirit through Scripture, creeds and liturgy. Christ's exercise of authority in the Church has centred 'around the issue of his communicable teaching' – on how we are to understand

and communicate, in doctrine and in deed, what Christ, through the Spirit abiding in the Church, shows us.

This brings up the sources of the Church's knowledge of Christ and here Scripture is 'the sovereign authority ... as the medium through which God by the Spirit communicates his word to the Church', enabling the response of understanding and of faith.[3] The Scriptures have to be understood and their meaning grasped through a continuing process of interpretation. By what principles and through what media? 'To this question Anglicanism has, since the seventeenth century, returned a straightforward, if broad and general, answer. Scripture is to be understood and read in the light afforded by the contexts of "tradition" and "reason".'[4] The section-report notes, as does classical Anglicanism, that the 'tradition' can denote *the faith once for all delivered to the saints* (the *hapax*), but that there is a wider sense, namely 'the ongoing, Spirit-guided life of the Church which receives, and in receiving interprets, God's message'. Thus, the Church appropriates the Scriptures, expressing its understanding and interpreting them in authoritative formulae 'which stand alongside the Scriptures themselves as summaries of their essential message'.[5] This is the familiar 'Scriptures and Creeds' as the doctrinal basis.

The document then goes on to analyse tradition as distinct from the classical formulae which this process of interpretation produces. Tradition in this sense is the growing 'mind' of the Church, *formed and challenged by the scriptural Word in the process of appropriating that Word in liturgy, life and teaching. The appeal to tradition is the appeal to this mind.*[6] Thus far, the modern statement and traditional Anglicanism are parallel. If one has a criticism of the Lambeth document it is that it does not really deal in detail with the nub of the question, namely, tradition's range of authority and the limits to the appeal to tradition. Certainly, both are distinctly implied by the primacy accorded to Scripture and by the statement that tradition and reason need each other. But the crunch-point for doctrinal authority and for the ecumenical dialogue arises when a dogma or practice is put forward as mandatory when its Scriptural basis is either not evident or at least open to serious question. While the document speaks rather blandly about the 'uncomfortable' dialogical situation when tradition and reason are in 'interplay and conflict',[7] it does not face up to the serious problem for the inter-Church dialogue of what traditional Anglicanism has always described as *dogmatic innovation* – a point constantly recurring in the course of our investigation. The Scriptural Word can at times challenge the 'mind' of the Church more acutely than Lambeth 1988 would appear to suggest.

When it comes to deal with reason the section-report describes it as a 'divine gift' and is crystal-clear on the necessity and validity of the threefold appeal for Christian authority as it discharges its primary task: 'Reason cannot be divorced either from Scripture or from tradition, since neither is even conceivable apart from the working of reason.'[8] Its essential role as a 'necessary instrument' for the interpretation of Scripture is plainly stated as part of the Anglican ethos.[9] We have earlier taken note of what the document defines as 'the interplay and conflict' between the common mind of the Church (tradition) and the common mind of a culture (reason) out of which the meaning of the Gospel for a particular time and place is discerned, a situation in which danger can arise if dialogue becomes monologue.[10] This is sound so long as 'reason' is not *solely* identified with the mind of a culture. In fact the section-report itself describes it as 'the divine gift' by which humans respond, as well as signifying 'that which is reasonable'. Traditional Anglicanism, as we have seen, keeps reminding us that reason is the capacity to ask for the evidence for a doctrine either in Scripture or in tradition. This is a warning which our own times dare not ignore, and not solely in respect of the priestly ordination of women. As A. S. McGrade writes: 'Reason has served Anglicans, and has often been explicitly invoked by them, as a counterpoise to unthinking biblicism or unthinking conformity to historical precedent.'[11] The main threats today from within to a credible authority in the Church come from unreasoning biblicism and from unreasoning traditionalism.

Apart from the riders (or perhaps footnotes?) which I have ventured to add by way of making more explicit the relation of Scripture to doctrinal innovation and the interplay of reason and tradition, what we have in this part of the section-report is a contemporary evaluation of authority. It is an assessment which neither invalidates nor ignores the previous history of Anglicanism, but sites it firmly in the modern ecumenical, multicultural and global context within which the Anglican Communion, in company with other fellow-Christians, proclaims the good news of the kingdom. It so relates the elements of authority to one another that tradition is seen to have limits, reason is recognized as a gift rather than an impersonal autonomy, and both circle round the uniquely fundamental Scriptures interpretatively and commentarially.

'The operation of authority in the Church is complex' as it discharges its primary function of nurturing the faithful in discipleship 'through a continuing process of interpretation, at the centre of which is the exposition of the Scriptures in the setting of the liturgy itself'. It is a process involving appeal to the settled mind of the Church (tradition) and to the standard of what is reasonable in the surrounding culture (reason): 'Inevitably the relationship between these different ways of reading the Scriptures, of understanding the mind of Christ, is strained.' Bearing in mind the section-report's earlier comment on the danger of monologue, one would remark that the strain is certainly inevitable if it is either/or that is implied by the phrase 'these different ways of reading the Scriptures'. One of the lessons to be learnt from classical Anglicanism is that tradition and reason must be used together in counter-balance as Scripture is interpreted – *they need each other*, as the report notes. In case of conflict it is authority's function 'to assure that when disagreement occurs it is settled in accord with the principles according to which Christians normally discern the mind of Christ for them: that the solution is rooted in Scripture, consonant with the mind of the Church, and "reasonable" in the sense that it speaks a language that the world can understand'. There are boundaries, and 'the point where the centre lies ... is Jesus Christ himself'.[12]

An immediate question then is whether the ordination of women can be set forth 'in terms of the will to pursue the mission of Jesus within the common framework of sacramental and scriptural discipline', or not. According to this Report 'no Province has argued the case as part of a wider rejection of the disciplines of Scripture and sacramental order'; and this raises the question, in the light of our study hitherto, as to what is the *actual basis* on which such ordinations are disallowed by some. Commenting that individual theologians are free to dissent, the section-report further records that 'no official Anglican body has promulgated a clear and unambiguous theological case against women's ordination'. This reflects the position noted by Lambeth 1978 that various Provinces had 'either agreed or approved in principle or stated that there are either no fundamental or no theological objections to the ordination of women to the historic threefold ministry of the Church'.[13]

It is of interest and bears on our theme that, in his most recent work, *Christianity* (1995), Hans Küng writes favourably on the Anglican Communion as a model to be followed and as a challenge to the persistence of the medieval paradigm. His comment is worthy of note here: 'Granted in some details we can note many deviations from the Anglican ideal. But there is no mistaking the fact that over the centuries this complex and relatively well-balanced church structure has largely proved itself, even in one of the most controversial of questions, the ordination of women.'[14]

The questions then must be whether it is the case that such ordination is consonant with Scripture and tradition, and what light is thrown by our study of the Anglican past and present on the application of the threefold appeal to this question, which for some is sufficiently divisive to be treated almost as if it were a fundamental of faith. What is the verdict of the Scriptures and what does tradition say? We have surely learnt that it is neither evasive nor disingenuous to observe that much depends on what you mean by 'Scripture' and by 'tradition'. If you are fundamentalist in either area you just *might* be able to believe, in spite of contradictions in the evidence, that there is no problem, on the grounds that 'the Bible says ...', or that 'tradition shows ...'. If, on the other hand, you have taken seriously the weight of the Anglican heritage and the thrust of the Anglican position, which is that Scripture and tradition cannot be separated from reason, then you find that major questions have to be asked and answered. You are in fact facing the reality of the necessity of Biblical hermeneutics and of the limits in the appeal to tradition. It is the contention of this study that this in fact is what is explicit and implicit in the formularies and formulations of the Anglican Communion, and that this is the effect and the meaning of the threefold appeal which is axiomatic for Anglican theology and within which the appeal to tradition has both its force and its limits.

X

An Application:
The Ordination of Women

If, then, the conviction is well founded that reason cannot be divorced from Scripture and tradition, we must try to discern the outcome of an application of this to the question of the priestly ordination of women, bearing in mind what we have uncovered concerning the balance of these three elements which is characteristic of Anglicanism. Nor, in this respect, is it question-begging if we remind ourselves here that constantly recurrent in the Anglican ethos is the distinction between the appeal to Scripture and biblicism, and between the appeal to tradition and traditionalism. The bearing of these three linked and basic concerns on the question in hand is, of course, obvious, and the thrust of them has been evident as being fundamental to the process of doctrinal authentication and the establishing of credible authority in the course of our investigation. If one were to take a text, so to speak, for this chapter, it might well be the words of Paul Avis, earlier quoted, on 'the place of reason, as competent to interpret scripture, adjudicate on tradition and instruct the Church as to *what was and what was not binding in both*'.

So, as Hooker, Laud, Taylor and Patrick put it, what is the nature of the evidence on which the Church has to judge and which it must interpret? First, is the Scriptural evidence clear, for or against? Straight away we are brought up against the matter of hermeneutics which we have seen to underlie the three points just noted. This comes to the fore at once, as in the title of a recent book by the Evangelical scholar, R. T. France: *Women in the Church's Ministry: A Test-case for Biblical Hermeneutics* (1995).

THE DOCTRINAL CONTEXT

However, before we look with reason on the evidence of Scripture and tradition we need to be aware of the real danger of getting things out of perspective by treating the ordination of women in isolation as if it were separately closed off by some kind of theological *cordon sanitaire*. As Christians, and irrespective of our viewpoint, we may not cease from seeing it in relation to the faith of the Gospel and in relation to the Community which lives by that faith. Two fundamental aspects of this Christian believing and belonging would appear to me to be the inescapable context within which the ordination of women must be considered, *the meaning of Christ's Sacred Humanity and the implications of baptism*. It is entirely pertinent that we should think of what we mean when we say that Christ took our humanity. This is where, for example, in a letter (1985) to Cardinal Jan Willebrands, the Archbishop of Canterbury located 'the most substantial doctrinal reason' justifying the ordination of women. Speaking of 'the fundamental principle of the Christian economy of salvation' when 'the Eternal Word assumed our flesh', Archbishop Runcie wrote: 'It is also common ground between us that the humanity taken by the Word, and now the risen and ascended humanity of the Lord of all creation, must be a humanity inclusive of women, if half the human race is to share in the Redemption he won for us on the Cross.' He then draws the conclusion that: 'Because the humanity of Christ our High Priest includes male and female, it is thus urged that the ministerial priesthood should now be open to women in order the more perfectly to represent Christ's inclusive High Priesthood.' The profound impact of this cannot be ignored in any assessment of the Scriptural evidence.

Of importance also in terms of the doctrinal context are the implications of baptism wherein, to quote the Prayer Book Catechism, 'I was made a member of Christ, the child of God, and an inheritor of the kingdom of Heaven'. That is to say, all that men and women are and have as Christians, their status, privileges and the graced fulfilling of responsibilities, comes to them 'through the washing of rebirth and renewal by the Holy Spirit' (Titus 3:5). The gifts and graces of the new life are conferred without distinction by the Spirit abiding in the Church: 'You are all sons of God through faith in Christ Jesus, for all of you who were baptised into Christ have been clothed with Christ. There is neither Jew nor Greek, slave nor free, male nor female, for you are all one in Christ Jesus' (Gal. 3:26–8). By virtue of union with Christ ratified in baptism the difference between male and female is irrelevant. It is sometimes suggested that this verse 'only applies to baptism', as if that ended the matter. Rather, does it not open up the whole matter, posing radical questions? Baptism means a total equality of discipleship, conferring 'that new personal identity which transcends the old identifying marks of humanity. Is one male or female, Jew or Gentile, in slavery or free? No, one is a new person in Christ. Nothing more fundamental can be said about anyone's life than that it has been lived as part of Christ's body.'[1] This, says Stephen Sykes, is the context in which ordination must be understood, and:

> in order to understand the relationship of baptism to ordination it is essential to distinguish between identity and role. To be a 'member' of Christ is a matter of identity; to be a priest is a matter of role ... no priest ever ceases to be a lay person. No one ever gets 'beyond' baptism. The ordained do not become 'super-members' of Christ.

In other words, what happens to us in baptism is the essential Christian vocation.

The role of the ministerial priesthood, according to ARCIC I, is to be a representative priesthood which is 'firmly placed in the context of the ministry of the whole Church and exists for the service of all the faithful', whose priesthood in turn 'is the consequence of incorporation by baptism into Christ'.[2] The priest is called upon to represent Christ but not to be a representation of Christ: 'An ambassador does not impersonate a monarch.'[3] In its Statement (1973) on ministry and ordination, ARCIC I strongly underlines the

intimate relation between this representative priesthood and
the universal priesthood of the baptised:

> Not only do they share through baptism in the priesthood of
> the people of God, but they are – particularly in presiding at
> the eucharist – representative of the whole Church in the fulfil-
> ment of its priestly vocation of self-offering to God as a living
> sacrifice (Rom. 12:1). Nevertheless their ministry is not an
> extension of the common priesthood but belongs to another
> realm of the gifts of the Spirit. It exists to help the Church to
> be 'a royal priesthood, a holy nation, God's own people, to
> declare the wonderful deeds of him who called [them] out of
> darkness into his marvellous light' (Pet. 2:9) [4]

In differing format, Sykes and the Commission are saying
much the same thing.

The pressing questions which arise from comparing the
view that 'the Church has no authority whatsoever to confer
priestly ordination on women' [5] with the foregoing have to
do with the nature of the Church and the work of the Spirit
abiding in the Church. If baptism confers the change of a
new identity on men and women alike, an identity which
makes gender irrelevant (Gal. 3), how or why, in spite of
such shared identity, is it allowable for only one section of
this universal priesthood to be called to the role of representative priesthood? We must endeavour to discern the reasons
for this blockage and for asserting its alleged impassability as
being 'in accordance with God's eternal plan' (*Apostolic
Letter*, 1994). If, as ARCIC I maintains, that priesthood is
distinct from the royal priesthood which it serves, then we
would appear to be saying not only that a woman cannot feel
such a vocation but that such a vocation does not require any
serious process of discernment. If a female member of the
Body of Christ experiences such a call is it a delusion? How
does this sit with the royal priesthood? More seriously still,
and indeed distressingly, we would seem to be saying that the
Spirit in the Church is in some way limited so that He cannot
inspire such a vocation, and more, that He cannot confer this
particular charism on a woman. Is it too much to say that
almost it looks as if we are saying that our institutional

adherence can constrain the Spirit? What theological grounds there are for this are hidden, and we shall try to investigate further, but here at this stage it reads as very strange doctrine. Are we being forced to ask whether, as Sister Lavinia Byrne put it, we are listening not to real theology but to the 'biology is destiny' tapes 'playing at full volume'? [6]

At this juncture it is apposite and directly relevant to our overall thesis on the nature of tradition to take note of the principles informing the decision-making of one Anglican Province, the Church of Ireland, which in 1990 chose over-whelmingly in favour of the ordination of women. The subject had been actively under consideration from 1977 when the General Synod had appointed a select committee to deal with 'the theological, practical, and other implications'. Study and discussion continued, culminating in a *Report* (1989) to the General Synod which led in the following year to the introduction and passing of a Bill requiring not less than two-thirds of each Order.[7]

The Introduction to the *Report* takes it as its starting point that all priesthood derives from Christ, whose priesthood 'is reflected in the royal priesthood of all the baptised and is focussed in the ordained priesthood of the Church', the task of the latter being 'to enable the royal priesthood of the baptised to realise its priestly vocation'. Significantly with reference to one of the matters raised earlier in this chapter, the *Report* observes: 'In the consideration of this question, *the role of the Holy Spirit* in guiding and directing the Church is of fundamental importance.'

The opening section of the *Report*, which sets out the arguments in favour and those against, comments that both views 'have implications for the way in which *authority* is both perceived and exercised in the Church', a point outlined throughout our early chapters. The *Report* then affirms the threefold source for the authority of the Church in 'faith and order, doctrine and development and worship and life'. It then explains and comments on the principles which should inform decision-making, and these are in fact the classical

Anglican stance applied to the questions 'whether a particular change of practice destroys or preserves the tradition' (§7), or whether such ordinations are 'a legitimate development' of the tradition, 'a natural extension of the sphere from which new members of the ordained ministry may be selected' (§13). The interaction of Scripture, Tradition and Reason is emphasized as the heart of the process, and 'the written word ... is the chief cornerstone of the Anglican position .... Scripture is the norm by which the Tradition and Reason are checked in matters of faith and practice' (§2–3). Classical Anglicanism is seen to be alive and well as the *Report* (§4) goes on to set the primacy of Scripture 'within the living Tradition of the Church' in the changing contemporary context when 'new questions are posed' which were never anticipated by the Primitive or the Medieval Church: 'To these questions, *self-evident* answers are not provided by Scripture and the received tradition.'

This *is the nub of the problem* and this is where reason is operative 'as an openness to the present and to the guidance of the Spirit', and as a corrective both to 'an understanding of the past which is fossilized and to the uncritical use of the Bible which ignores the principles of sound exegesis'. In other words, a modern Anglican statement is affirming a hermeneutic as essential and is rejecting traditionalism and biblicism. This resonates with all that we have been uncovering in the Anglican ethos past and present. Nor is reason an autonomy, but it 'concerns coherence and faithfulness to that which is and has been received. It seeks the mind of the Holy Spirit and is therefore the fruit of the whole Christian community. In short Reason is the continuing reflection upon Scripture and Tradition in the light of contemporary experience' (§6). Finally, in a paragraph meriting quotation in full, the *Report* (§15) underlines the value of tradition and of the Early Church's witness in the context of the unceasing work of the Spirit abiding in the Church:

> Anglicans have always placed a particular value on the appeal to the life and witness of the primitive Church, to the Creeds, and to the decisions of the Ecumenical Councils.

By 'Tradition' is understood the faith of the ages as it has reflected upon and interpreted the message of Scripture in the life of the Church and in the world, and thus it is seen as *dynamic not static*. This provides an acknowledged corrective within Anglicanism to private opinion or subjective and situational responses to Scripture. Tradition is not set over against Scripture, but is the ongoing witness and work of the Holy Spirit in the Church seeking both to recall and renew all things in Christ.

We call to mind the words of Olivier Clément: 'Tradition is not a written text ... it is the expression of the Spirit *juvenescens*' – for the Spirit in the Church is ever in his youthfulness. It has been thought useful to give some space to this *Report*, bringing as it does the classical Anglican approach into the contemporary scene, since, although it was published in the *General Synod 1989 Reports*, it will not be widely known.

The thrust of these working principles is quite simply that *here* is the natural *point de départ* for Anglicans assessing this question: '*The context of the discussion is set out ... as being clearly that of Scripture, Tradition and Reason, and constant reference has been made to the Preamble and Declaration to which this Church is committed*' (§104). Not from fundamentalism or traditionalism, both of which are deeply anticritical and so not native to a Church which has always explicitly treasured sound learning in the exposition of the Faith, can convincing positions be established. In September 1996, the Archbishop of Wales made it explicit that the basis undergirding the decision by the Church in Wales in favour of the priestly ordination of women was the threefold Anglican criterion of Scripture, tradition and reason.

So, what is, and is not, binding in Scripture and tradition?

THE EVIDENCE OF SCRIPTURE

'The sense of the Church is not a rule; but a thing ruled. The Church is bound unto reason and Scripture, and governed by them as much as any particular person.' Bearing in mind this comment by Whichcote, we must now reflect on the implications of the Biblical texts, endeavouring to handle the matter with integrity and sensitivity. Since the Scriptures constitute 'the real origins', the criterion of authenticity, can we find in them, taken as a whole, a positive and self-evident directive? If something is declared to be *mandatory* in the life of the Spirit-led community, it should be clear in Scripture, consonant with the content and thrust of the Gospel and not one of the uncertain or disputed questions, for Scripture is 'the vital, binding norm for the Christian Church of all times' (Küng, *Infallibility?*). The Church has no way of deciding this question but by reason and by being open to the Spirit both in *recalling* and in *renewing* the life of the Church as it relates the faith of the ages to its contemporary experience. From the beginning, Anglicanism has been seen to reject the line that the teaching of the *magisterium*, the 'living teaching authority', is, in the words of the SCDF *Commentary* (pp. 4, 13), 'the point of departure' and 'ensures discernment between what can change and what must remain immutable'. The Anglican formularies and theologians we have been examining consistently repudiate this, insisting that the sense of the Church is not a rule but is ruled by Scripture and reason. In other words, reason and Scripture and tradition need each other in the ongoing interpretation and explication of the Faith once for all delivered.

It is a standpoint taken by some that the fact of the all-male apostolate puts any question of the ministry of women in the Church out of court. The basis of this requires examination. Significantly for the development of the tradition it was only after the third century that this argument began to be used. There can obviously be no question but that Jesus chose twelve men. He *did* this, but it does not therefore follow as a deduction that He was thereby laying down a *law* for all time. Hooker warned that 'when that which the word of God doth but deliver *historically*, we construe without any warrant as if it were *legally meant*' then we are adding to Scripture. It is quite inadequate simply to say 'that this call was made in accordance with God's eternal plan' (*Apostolic Letter* of Pope John Paul II, 1994), or that 'The real reason is that ... Christ established things in this way' (Address by Pope Paul VI, 1977). This is merely to *assert*, although the Pontifical Commission had informed Paul VI that, in their opinion, 'there was no valid biblical reason for opposing the ordination of women to the priesthood'.[8] The appointment of the twelve did not happen in some sort of space/time vacuum. Christianity is above all a historical religion. The Son of God assumed our humanity at a certain time, 'the fulness of time', and in the context of a specific culture. That culture was one in which women were not only societally subordinate but ideologically inferior to men.

The Levitical code was markedly discriminatory, particularly in respect of women's ritual 'uncleanness', and daughters were inferior to sons in the family, nor did they have the latter's rights. A Jewish male was expected daily to thank God that he was not born a Gentile, a slave, or a woman. In his careful study, *Why No Women Priests?* (1988), Gilbert Wilson, formerly Bishop of Kilmore, has gone very thoroughly into the influence of Jewish cultural factors. Pointing out that their inferior status prevented women from going beyond the Court of the Women in the Temple, he notes that while they were permitted to attend the weekly synagogue service they were separated from the men and they were deliberately deprived of opportunities for studying the *Torah*, so important to Jews 'as a source of spiritual life and way of salvation'. Some of this passed over into the thinking of the Christian Fathers and obliges us to consider the sources of the 'constant practice of the Church, which has imitated Christ in choosing only men ... and ... the example recorded in the Sacred Scriptures of Christ choosing his Apostles only from among men' (Papal reply to letter of 1975 from Archbishop Coggan of Canterbury to Paul VI).[9] The same letter affirms that the living teaching authority of the Church continues to exclude women from the priesthood, and claims, without any attempt to study the factors which created the tradition, that this is in accordance with God's plan for the Church.

But 'the sense of the Church is not a rule; but a thing ruled'. If we are 'bound unto reason and Scripture' this is where Scripture and tradition cannot be divorced from reason. So, we are obliged to ask, did Jesus choose men as apostles because an effectual leadership had to be acceptable to contemporaries and able to teach in the synagogues *or* because women *by their very nature* could not be considered for apostleship? We are back to hermeneutics when we insist that it is against reason to disregard the influence of the cultural *milieu*, and when we claim that there is no evidence that the choice of a male apostolate was in the nature of a law of Christ binding the Church's choice of ministry in perpetuity. If the assumptions about the inferior status of women are now neither demonstrable nor acceptable, 'the appeal to tradition is virtually reduced to the observation that there happened to be no precedent for ordaining women to be priests. The New Testament does not encourage Christians to think that nothing should be done for the first time'.[10] We remember Hooker's words, 'All things cannot be of ancient continuance, which are expedient and needful for the ordering of spiritual affairs' – anticipating this comment by Lambeth 1968.

What is at the heart of the question here is not the authority of Scripture but the right way to interpret and apply it. R. T. France suggests that conflicting views on the ordination of women stem in the first place

> from two different hermeneutical approaches, the one focusing on certain passages and strands of the New Testament which suggest that there is a permanent God-given distinction between the roles of men and women which rules out the exercise of teaching and authority by women, while the other appeals to the wider scriptural pattern and also questions whether apostolic rulings for first-century church situations should be applied in the same way to the very different church scene of twentieth-century Europe.[11]

As I see it, certain matters crowd to the surface here and they are interlinked. There is the analysis of the small number of passages over against the trajectory of the attitude to women in the Scriptures. Connected with this is the question as to whether Hooker's 'new-grown occasion' is upon us, seeing that the belief in the natural inferiority of women, now discredited, is deeply embedded in the tradition from Judaism and from many of the patristic writers through the medieval period to the present. Furthermore, if tradition is dynamic and not static, must a practice evolved in a particular cultural setting be treated as immutable? Moreover, is it not tendentious selectivity to claim that tradition can only be preserved by forbidding change in respect of the ordination of women when, as Jewel pointed out long ago, the *dominical* tradition of communion in both kinds was reversed?

If we turn to the total witness of the Scriptures in respect of the role of women in the New Testament Church it becomes clear that judgments have to be made. As Jeremy Taylor wrote, 'reason is the judge' when we find that self-evident answers are not provided or when deductions from the evidence are open to the influence of cultural bias. Apart from the passage in 1 Timothy 2:8–15 which clearly focuses on the subject and, to a lesser degree, 1 Corinthians 14:34–5, to both of which we must return, what do we learn from the Epistles and the Acts about the place and activity of women in the first-century Church? What light does such an examination throw on the tradition of an all-male priesthood, its origin and its validity for the Church at the close of the twentieth century? From the point of view of the theme of this book, does the Scripture (which controls tradition) give decisive answers? Is the evidence for the tradition clear and conclusive or was Nicholas Lash, writing recently in *The Tablet* on the Vatican decree excluding women from the ordained ministry in his Church, correct when he concluded that the evidence from Scripture against the ordination of women is simply not compelling?

Our study heretofore from Hooker onwards has shown that to be guided by Scripture, to be faithful to the authority of Scripture, involves interpretation. A hermeneutic is required in which faithfulness to the Bible is not defined in terms of an immutable fundamentalism in respect of the Biblical texts, or rather a selection from them. This particular standpoint can find itself in very equivocal situations as the New Testament story unfolds and as evidence from early mosaics, inscriptions and epitaphs reveals that all was not in fact as some supporters of the exclusion of women from the Church's ministry have presented the tradition, namely, as obtaining always, everywhere and received by all.

By way of illustration, one may ask with R. T. France 'What really was going on in the Pauline churches?'[12] It is a question handled in detail by Karen Jo Torjesen in her book *When Women were Priests* (1993), by Ruth B. Edwards in *The Case for Women's Ministry* (1989), and by many others, notably Hans Küng in *The Church* (1967). So, what is the evidence of Scripture on which the Church has to make judgment? In the churches at Rome, Corinth, Philippi and elsewhere we find women exercising roles in worship and in ministry and they are treated as partners in the work by Paul. Although he accepts as something given the male-orientated society of the Greek and Roman as well as the Jewish world, just as he accepts the institution of slavery, he describes these women as *synergoi*, fellow-workers. Such were Euodia and Syntyche (Phil. 4:2), Mary and Persis (Rom. 16:6), Tryphena and Tryphosa (Rom. 16:12). Priscilla with her husband Aquila are Paul's *synergoi en Christō Iēsou*, and he clearly endorses her teaching ministry to men like Apollos (cf. Acts 18:24-6). Then there was Junia, 'outstanding among the apostles' (Rom. 16:7), and Phoebe, *diakonos* of the church in Cenchreae (Rom. 16:1).

One has to wonder whether the words *synergos*, *diakonos* and *apostolos* lose their ordinary meaning when applied to women. Clearly, these women and others mentioned were more deeply involved in the mission of the Church than just tidying up after the *agapē*! On the contrary, says Paul, 'they worked very hard in the Lord' and 'all the Churches of the Gentiles are grateful to them'. Phoebe was not only *diakonos* in Cenchreae but she brought Paul's letter to Rome and he introduces her as his *prostatis*, meaning 'patron' or 'chief'.

Junia was, with her husband Andronicus, a travelling teacher and preacher who met Paul in prison: 'She was a heroine of the fourth-century Christian church, and John Chrysostom's elegant sermons invoked the image of Junia, the apostle, for the Christian women of Constantinople to emulate.'[13] Everyone from Origen to Abelard realised that Junia 'the apostle' was a woman in spite of the efforts of some modern commentators to render the name as the masculine Junias, a form which apparently in fact has never occurred.[14] Acts 21:8–9 recounts Paul's stay 'at the house of Philip the evangelist, one of the Seven' who had four daughters who exercised the charism of prophesying.

What then does Scripture say that these women were doing? They were exercising an active ministry, travelling, prophesying and teaching. Moreover, they were praying and prophesying in church, evidently with Paul's approval (1 Cor. 11:5), which makes all the more puzzling his demand in the same letter (1 Cor. 14:34–5) that they should be silent in church and 'in submission as the Law says'. It has been debated whether these verses really belong here and as to what kind of speaking – with tongues, or prophesying, or just talking 'out of place' – is meant here by *laleō*, especially since the passage contradicts what the same letter says about women's role in worship and all that is implied in Romans 16. Whatever the truth of this textual matter may be, it still leaves us with Paul, who holds to the female-submission view of society, nevertheless pursuing a ministerial partnership with women in the ministry of the Gospel.

It may be objected at this point that whatever they were, they were not priests. But then, in the Pauline churches who was? Paul's letters never refer to *presbuteroi* or indeed to ordination, and his only reference to bishops is in the plural, the *episkopoi* and *diakonoi* of Philippians 1:1. We do not know if women were among the former in the church at Philippi but we do know that Phoebe was *diakonos* in the church at Cenchreae. It is simply anachronistic to impose on the fluid and diverse situation of the Pauline communities the more structured picture of ministry beginning to emerge in the Acts, the pastoral epistles and the Ignatian letters. 'We realize today,' wrote E. P. Echlin, 'that there was a pluralism of mutually recognized ministries in the early Church which coexisted in full communion.' The fact is that the New Testament nowhere lays down an exclusive pattern of ministry, revealing as it does elements of episcopal, presbyteral, congregational and charismatic forms of ministry. Edwards' conclusion is just: 'There is nothing in the New Testament ideals and practice of ministry which in itself should exclude women from it, but rather many features which endorse and encourage their participation.' Significantly, she notes that Anglican and Roman Catholic theologians including Hanson, Küng, Schillebeeckx and Boff concur, and she comments, 'the barriers which have been perceived stem from particular attitudes towards the male apostolate and other ministries, and from developments in the Church's understanding of ministry in post-biblical times'.[15]

The bearing of this on the basic thesis being advanced in this book is that the evidence from Scripture is neither conclusive nor indeed compelling, for the view that an exclusively male priesthood is part of God's eternal plan so that the Church has no authority whatsoever to confer priestly ordination on women. Consequently, the tradition itself is deficient in authority and its origins and force must be sought elsewhere when today's Church looks with reason on Scripture and tradition in order to decide what is and what is not binding in both.

1 TIMOTHY 2:8–15

Two other aspects of the Scriptural evidence remain to be considered, namely, the passage from 1 Timothy 2:8–15, characterized as 'the storm-centre of debate' by R. T. France, and the implications for ministry of the house-churches, *hē kat' oikon ekklēsia* of 1 Corinthians 16:19, Colossians 4:15 and Philemon 2.

There is, of course, the question of the Pauline authorship

of 1 Timothy. But whether we side with, for example, John Robinson who regarded it as genuine and dated 55 AD[16] or with those who reject the ascription to Paul on grounds of style, vocabulary and doctrine and as revealing a ministerial structure and church organization suited to the early decades of the following century, the fact remains that, like the textually uncertain 1 Corinthians 14:34–5, the passage contradicts 1 Corinthians 11:5 and the whole range of Paul's ministerial partnership with women. The bearing of this contradiction on the nature of the overall Scriptural evidence and on the basis for the tradition needs little stressing.

Much has been written, from both sides of the debate, on the exegesis of this passage. Without attempting to go into too much detail on a passage which has produced much analysis and no little controversy among specialists in New Testament studies, possibly the real question from the point of view of this book is: Can it be shown that these verses constitute an unbreakable law for the Church, seeing that they contradict all that is to be learnt from Galatians, 1 Corinthians and Romans? In his *Gospel and Spirit* (1991), G. D. Fee puts the matter concisely: 'It is hard to deny that *this* text prohibits women teaching men in the Ephesian church; but it is the unique text in the New Testament, and as we have seen its reason for being is *not* to correct the rest of the New Testament, but to correct a very ad hoc problem in Ephesus.'[17] The city of Ephesus was the centre of the Artemis-cult with its predominantly female priesthood. Was Paul (or the author) striving to distance the local church from this threatening ambience by forbidding women to teach? If there is truth in this then this solitary passage can hardly be a rule for a global Church in the twentieth century. Again it has been suggested that the opponents referred to in the letter may well have been some type of the ascetic gnosticism then common: 'They forbid people to marry and order them to abstain from certain foods' (1 Tim. 4:3).

This would explain the prominence of inter-sex relationships in the letter, and France quotes D. M. Scholer's view that 'the problem ... was with women who were being influenced by this ascetic-gnosticizing movement within the church to despise marriage and to aspire instead to roles in the life of the church for which they were not equipped'; and he quotes: 'It addresses a particular situation of false teaching in Ephesus that assaulted and abused what was considered appropriate and honorable behavior for women.'[18] The concern then of the passage would be with the correct and fitting role of 'a wife in relation to her husband in the context of worship. If that is the case, there must be a question-mark against the use of this passage as a general prescription for the respective roles of men and women in worship, irrespective of the marriage relationship'.[19] This interpretation is surely supported by the author's use of Adam and Eve in the Creation narrative as the pattern of marriage, but using the Jewish exegesis which regarded Eve as responsible for the Fall (1 Tim. 2:13–15), a line followed in many patristic writings. It should be noted that elsewhere, as in Romans 5 and 1 Corinthians 15, Paul ascribes the Fall to Adam, making no mention of Eve. The bearing of this on the question of the authorship of 1 Timothy is another point well worthy of consideration. Apart from this, do we *still* have to remind ourselves that the Fall narrative of Genesis 3, used constantly through the centuries until today as a basis for the subordination of women, is not history but myth, a story with a theological purpose?

The latest contribution to Pauline scholarship, Jerome Murphy-O'Connor's *Paul, A Critical Life* (1996), concurs that neither 1 Corinthians 14:34–5 nor 1 Timothy are the work of the apostle. He argues that the Pastorals differ from the other letters of the Pauline corpus in respect of language, style, theological perspective, church organization and the kind of opposition faced by the church. Recognizing the affinity of 1 Timothy and Titus, he concludes that critics are justified in the view that 2 Timothy could not be the product of the same author and could be regarded as being more 'at home in the Pauline corpus'. The thrust here, however, is to show that Paul's view of women's status is not that of 1 Timothy 2:11–14, and that 1 Corinthians 14:34–5 was 'added by a later hand to bring it into line with the non-Pauline 1 Tim. 2:11–14'.

Murphy-O'Connor, dealing with 'the confusion at Corinth' gives this analysis:

> Aware, however, that Genesis 2:21–2 was used in Jewish circles to demonstrate the inferiority and subordination of women, Paul immediately moved to ensure that nothing more than what he intended could be drawn from his premiss. 1 Corinthians 11:11–12 is the first and only explicit defence of the complete equality of women in the New Testament. Paul overturned the traditional argument from the chronological priority of the male in the creation narrative by pointing out that the chronological priority of woman in the birth of a male is just as much part of God's plan for the order of his creation (1 Cor. 11:12). This elementary argument functions as proof for the principle, 'As Christians, woman is not otherwise than man, and man is not otherwise than woman' (v. 11). *Equality is the issue here, not complementarity.* The strength and clarity of this insight means that the directive that women must keep silent in church (1 Cor. 14:34–5) cannot come from the pen of Paul.

Most significantly for the thesis which I advance in this chapter, the author, who is a Dominican priest and professor of New Testament at the École Biblique in Jerusalem, writes of women's ministry:

> Paul took it entirely for granted that women were ministers of the church in precisely the same sense as men. He recognized their gifts as fruits of the Spirit, which he had neither the desire nor the authority to oppose. Given the androcentric world in which he lived, however, it would be surprising if there were not stirrings of opposition among those who failed to appreciate just how radical the gospel was.[20]

Even were the Pauline authorship insisted upon it would appear to me that the same inference and implications remain. Is not the claim that Scripture excludes women from the priesthood invalidated since *in fact* the Scriptural evidence as a whole points to two opposite conclusions? It amounts to choosing Paul's teaching and practice or the ruling of 1 Timothy. To admit that there is a choice is to concede that the ministerial exclusion of women is neither a Scriptural mandate nor the incontrovertible message of the total Scriptures. Equally, the assertion is negated that an exclusively male priesthood is and has been part of the eternal plan for the Church, since *in fact* there was a ministry of women at the beginning of the Church's mission. 'If we must judge, then we must use our reason,' wrote Jeremy Taylor, dealing with precisely such circumstances when the evidence, either from Scripture or tradition, appears contrary. As noted at the beginning of this chapter and throughout our investigation, reason cannot be divorced from Scripture and tradition. A hermeneutic is a simple necessity. Otherwise biblicism and traditionalism become autonomous and an end in themselves, replacing the living dialogue between Scripture and tradition and the response of reception which are ongoing in the life of the Community in which the Spirit abides.

All this throws light on why this sole passage contradicts the rest of the Epistles. It also explains why, when we look with reason on Scripture and when we move from exegesis to hermeneutics, we cannot regard this solitary passage, with its ambiguities (for example, the meaning here of *authentēo*) and its openness to a variety of interpretation, as a certain and adequate basis for a ruling which binds the Church in all ages and places. What does this say about the origin and the force of the tradition?

THE HOUSE CHURCHES

The significance of the house churches for the spreading of the Gospel and the building up of the new Community is clear in the New Testament. Schüssler Fiorenza notes that 'house churches were a decisive factor in the missionary movement insofar as they provided space, support, and actual leadership for the community. The house churches were the place where the early Christians celebrated the Lord's supper and preached the good news.' [21] There is much that is illuminating and informative about the house churches in Jerome Murphy-O'Connor's study of Paul, his life and times (pp. 149–51). He makes clear the importance of their role in Paul's mission, their composition and the kind of people whose houses became centres of worship. He addresses the question of Gentile and Jewish house churches within the *ecclesia* and how the problem of table-fellowship would have been managed. Not many of the converts would have belonged to the social level which had large dwellings. Inevitably, as the Christian community grew there would have been a number of house churches in any given city such as Antioch. Gaius, 'whose hospitality I and the whole church here enjoy' (Rom. 16:23), was probably wealthier than most believers since only a large house would accommodate the entire community. These were the settings and this was the sphere which made it possible for women to take a prominent part in the life of the nascent Church. Thus, we read of Aphia, 'our sister', who was a leader in the house church in Colossae (Philem. 2). There were Prisca and Aquila and 'the church in their house' (1 Cor. 16:19; Rom. 16:5), and Nympha of Laodicea and 'the church in her house' (Col. 4:15). Acts 16:15 tells of Lydia, the first convert in Europe, whose house became a centre for the young Church. The disciples in Jerusalem met in the house of Mary, John Mark's mother (Acts 12:12).

The bearing of the house churches on the ministry of women in the infant Church arises from the sharp distinction made in the ancient world between private and public space. In spite of the accepted model of female subordination in society as a whole, women were regarded as having authority in the private sphere of the household, the public sphere being male territory. When the church was located in the house, this gave women the opportunity of leadership, and indeed one remembers that Paul called the Church 'the household of faith' (Gal. 6:10). This situation lies behind the prominence of women in the beginning of the Christian mission. Torjesen comments:

> So long as church leadership continued to model itself on the familiar role of household manager, there was no cultural

barrier to women assuming leadership roles. First- and second-century Christians, familiar with the authority and leadership role of the female head of household, would have perceived women's leadership within the church as not only acceptable but natural .... This would have been the case as long as Christian communities remained closely identified with the social structures of the private sphere.[22]

The ambivalence seen in the New Testament writings as between the subordinationist view of women in society and the more liberal situation in the early Christian communities, fostered by the house churches and inspired by the teaching of Jesus and his attitude to women, began to be replaced from the middle of the third century by an understanding of church office as totally male-centred. Once the church moved into public space the pressure to conform to the pattern of society and to adopt the model of civic leadership was overwhelming, thus legitimizing the church in public opinion – it isn't wise to be different! The imposition of the stereotype was not however accomplished without controversy; but as monarchical episcopacy continued to develop, and as the church finally went public by moving into basilicas, by the fourth century the male leadership model of the Roman city council finally replaced the more fluid early situation:

> As Christianity entered the public sphere, male leaders began to demand the same subjugation of women in the churches as prevailed in Greco-Roman society at large. Their detractors reproached women leaders, often in strident rhetoric, for operating outside the domestic sphere and thus violating their nature and society's vital moral codes. How could they remain virtuous women, the critics demanded, while being active in public life? [23]

What took place gradually was a process of institutionalizing and structuralization made necessary indeed by the very success of the Gospel mission to the world and by the growth of the Church. As always, the process reflects the milieu in which it develops, and in this case the assimilation reflected the cultural norms of the society in which the Church was at work, a society which held that public office was a male preserve. What was taking place over the period was, in Schüssler Fiorenza's aphoristic phrase 'the genderization of ecclesial office'.[24] During the first three centuries the question was hotly debated, both sides arguing even at this early stage from 1 Timothy 2 and Galatians 3:28 respectively, from women being of an inferior nature and from men and women having the same nature.[25] Nevertheless, as the house churches gradually turned into the church in the public sphere, the argument from the prevailing gender ideology of contemporary society proved increasingly effective and women, in spite of their roles in the apostolic Church, became more and more marginalized in the life of the Christian communities. This brief historical sketch, while far from being an inclusive and comprehensive picture, seems to be an accurate presentation and unlikely to be factually faulted in its essentials. The question then is: In the light of the Scriptural evidence and that of the post-apostolic church, how is it possible to claim that an exclusively male priesthood is in accordance with God's plan for the Church? Are we thinking in terms of history and serious theology or some kind of *midrashim*?

TESTING THE TRADITION

The advice of Simon Patrick is as necessary and as cogent as ever it was: four tests must be applied in order to authenticate a tradition – its origin, content, authority and verifiability. He values and venerates tradition when it is an unfolding and an explanation of the meaning of Scripture, and he adds, 'we admit all other traditions which are subordinate and agreeable unto that; together with all those things that can be proved to be apostolical by the general testimony of the Church in all ages'. In the same vein, Hooker before him had affirmed of traditions that 'we do not reject them only because they are not in Scripture, but because they are neither in Scripture, *nor can otherwise sufficiently be proved to be of God*'. We are thus being advised to test the tradition by agreement with Scripture, by apostolicity and by asking ourselves if it is verifiably a divine ordinance, in accordance with God's eternal plan. In other words, any tradition must be tested by Scripture and reason to establish whether it is or is not binding on the Church.

What does this appear to be saying in respect of the present debate? Is it not that, if the evidence of Scripture provides no conclusive and compelling proof that the exclusion of women from priesthood is an unquestioned and immutable law from apostolic times onward nor, moreover, that it is revealed as a divinely-ordered plan for the life of the Church, then whence comes the tradition and from where does it derive the authority which makes it mandatory for the Church Catholic in every generation? The answer would seem to lie in 'development in the Church's understanding of ministry in post-biblical times',[26] something of which we have already taken note. It is generally agreed that a contributory factor here was the prejudiced attitude among the Fathers to women and their extolling of virginity as a superior state to marriage. This was noted early on by Jewel, who had made a distinction between needing 'oftentimes the discretion and wisedome of the Learned Fathers' in interpreting the Scriptures on the one hand, and in secondary matters on the other, when 'savinge the reverence dewe unto them, we may well reprove or refuse some things in their writings'. Such a case he instances when 'Diverse the Holy Fathers have written over basely I wil not saie, vilely, and sclaunderously of the state of Matrimonie in general.'[27]

Needless to say, the evidence varies, but the general attitude to women in the patristic writings would appear to be based firmly on the current view of female subordination and on the creation narratives so interpreted. These were interpreted along the line of the Jewish tradition which laid the responsibility of the Fall on Eve. This ties in with the further point, made by many scholars, that the asceticism of the Fathers created – as for example, in Augustine after his conversion – a 'fear of the feminine extended even to relations within marriage'.[28] Wilson concurs, linking this observable patristic *weltanschauung* with the early encouragement of celibacy as a more spiritual state than matrimony and with the fourth-century development of Eastern monasticism. Side by side with this in the West was the continuing effort to enforce clerical celibacy from the end of the fourth century until despite resistance it became a universal decree (but never accepted in the East) in the eleventh and twelfth centuries, although the Council of Nicaea had earlier rejected a similar proposal. All this ran counter to the tradition of a married apostolate of 1 Corinthians 9:4 and a married ministry of 1 Timothy 3:2–12, and was so noted by the Council of Trullo in 692: 'We, observing the ancient canon of apostolical perfection and order, declare that the marriages of all in holy orders are to be henceforth accounted valid, and we refuse to forbid cohabitation.' [29]

What we are talking about is the progressive creation of an ecclesial climate through a combination of the cultural and the theological, the subordinate status of women in society and the literalist (and at times misogynistic) exegesis in subordinationist terms of passages such as Genesis 3. The denunciations of Epiphanius in the fourth century are an indication, and not a solitary case, of how hostile this climate was to women's ministry, and *The Statutes of the Apostles* similarly excluded them from presiding at the Eucharist because of their nature.[30] An honourable exception to the prevailing trend was John Chrysostom, who granted that women could exercise ministry though it might not be expedient: 'If he knew of any theological reason why women should be considered *ineligible* for priesthood, it is remarkable that he did not mention it, rather than say it could be done "even by women" ', particularly as this was written in his book *On the Priesthood*.[31]

Any candid evaluation of the state of the question must also take account of the implications of the evidence for what Lavinia Byrne calls the hidden tradition, though some writers prefer the adjective 'repressed'. Many people are aware of the second- or third-century fresco in the Greek Chapel of the Priscilla Catacomb in Rome, in which a woman breaks bread at the Eucharist, in company with six other figures grouped around a table. But not everyone knows that:

> when the archaeologist Joseph Wilpert discovered this fresco in the nineteenth century he commissioned a water-colour reproduction of it. The artist who made a copy of this scene for the archives of the Pontifical Commission of Sacred Archaeology actually firmed up the evidence by adding manly thighs and a beard to the figure closest to us and made sure the others looked like real men – bar the veiled figure of the real/proper/natural woman.[32]

What one may call this gender-manipulation of evidence was not confined to later times. There is the beautiful mosaic over a chapel doorway in the Basilica of St Prassede in Rome. In it are depicted with circular haloes Mary and the saints Praxedis and Prudentiana. On the left is a fourth woman with a square halo (indicating that she was then alive), and over her head and to the side is the lettering 'Episcopa Theodora'. The final 'a' of her name has been partially scratched out on the mosaic, a piece of gender-editing which may have been done many centuries ago. Lavinia Byrne records other inscriptions 'uncovered over the past century. Fifteen of these so far, from ancient Gaul to Cappadocia, recall the work of women priests.'[33] She provides further instances including a disapproving letter of the fifth-century Pope Gelasius I, from which is made clear the fact that some women were officiating at the altar. We may round off this brief aside on the supportive 'positive' evidence from inscriptions and epitaphs which meshes in with the supportive 'negative' evidence from patristic writings with a note by Torjesen:

> Giorgio Otranto, an Italian professor of church history, has shown through papal letters and inscriptions that women participated in the Catholic priesthood for the first thousand years of the church's history. The last thirty years of American scholarship have produced an amazing range of evidence for women's roles as deacons, priests, presbyters, and even bishops in Christian churches from the first through the thirteenth century.[34]

Otranto's phrase concerning 'a repression' of historical sources cannot be ignored as one seeks for the origin, authority and verifiability of the tradition of an exclusively male priesthood. It is difficult to avoid the conclusion that the tradition stems from the merger between patristic teaching on women and their subordinate social status. Underlying this merger, and explicitly stated from the formative period of the Fathers to the twelfth-century *Decree* of Gratian which formalized the exclusion of women from ordination, was the belief that by her *very nature* woman is inferior to man. This received its final *imprimatur* in the *Summa* of Aquinas as the reason why a woman cannot be ordained. It is worth pausing to evaluate St Thomas's argument as here the weakness of the case becomes evident. It appears to rest on two affirmations which are in fact assumptions, namely, the necessity of maleness for the valid conferral of the sacrament of Order, and the inferiority, the subjection in nature, of woman. Not surprisingly, he begins his presentation with 1 Timothy 2:12, but loosely conflated with the words 'in the Church' from 1 Corinthians 14:34. Dismissing Old Testament examples of women prophets on the grounds that 'prophecy is not a sacrament but a gift of God', Aquinas then asserts that the 'signification' of maleness is essential to the sacrament of Order. This he combines with the female 'state of subjection' to exclude women from the priesthood, though he permits some diaconal functions.

It seems best to allow the passage to speak for itself:

> Accordingly we must say that the male sex is required for receiving Orders not only in the second but also in the first way [i.e. in respect both of 'lawfulness' and of 'validity']. Wherefore even though a woman were made the object of all that is done in conferring Orders, she would not receive Orders, for since a sacrament is a sign, *not only of the thing, but the signification of the thing*, is required in all sacramental actions; thus it was stated above that in Extreme Unction it is necessary to have a sick man, in order to signify the need of healing. Accordingly, since it is not possible in the female sex to *signify eminence of degree*, for a woman is in *the state of subjection*, it follows that she cannot receive the sacrament of Order.[35]

What we have here is a theology of this sacrament and an interpretation of the human condition both of which depend for their validation on a gender-assumption, all the more shaky as a basis in experience and reality in view of his admission that 'sometimes a woman is found to be better than many men as regards the soul'. The deduction which follows in the concluding Reply is that a woman can receive the charism of prophecy but not the sacrament of Orders because, though she 'does not differ from man as to the thing' she differs in 'the signification'. The argument illustrates how for Aquinas the exclusively male tradition of priesthood is inextricably involved with an Aristotelian physiology and psychology which no longer make sense medically or empirically.

No matter how the apologia is phrased or varied today something of this element lies behind the presentation of the case against the priestly ordination of women. It was the detection of a degree of official unease concerning this factor which prompted the criticism by Stephen Sykes of the *Declaration* and the *Commentary* in his essay referred to earlier:

> But both publications are characterised by an extreme reluctance to present an historical picture of the traditional scholastic synthesis, claiming that 'the undeniable influence of prejudices unfavourable to women' or the presence of arguments 'that modern thought would have difficulty in admitting or would even rightly reject' can be easily separated from the Church's constant tradition. *One can have no such confidence.*[36]

With this conclusion our investigation hitherto would concur.

All this is a far cry from the implications for shared identity of membership in the Body of Christ which many think may justly, or even necessarily, be drawn from the doctrine of the Sacred Humanity and from the work of the Spirit in baptism. Be that as it may, the evidence which we have been considering from a variety of sources certainly subserves the general position on the origins and authority of traditions in the Church which this study endeavours to present. It is an endeavour to call to mind from the Anglican past and present a valid methodology for handling tradition. Out of and by means of the threefold appeal it attempts to furnish a sound theological basis for an open and candid answer to the question of women's ordination, a basis which 'refuses to insulate itself against the testing of history and the free action of reason'. Last at the Cross, first at the Tomb, but never at the Altar – Why?

TRADITION, CHANGE AND HISTORICITY

A distinguished dignitary of the Roman Catholic Church once said to me in the course of a conversation, 'I would have no problem with the ordination of women if the Church decided for it.' While on the superficial level this might be dismissed as what is nowadays termed a cop-out, such was *not* my friend's intention. It was a serious discussion and he was saying two things that bear on our investigation. He was implying that tradition can change and is not an immutable, a view always maintained by Anglicans. He was also implying that the sentence of the present Church is the inerrant *point de départ*, a view consistently rejected by Anglicans as enshrined in Article XIX, which states that Churches can err and have erred 'in their living and manner of Ceremonies, and also in matters of Faith'.

The reality is that the history of the Church shows tradition to be open both to deliberate selectivity and to the evolving process of change. The classic instance of the former is the withdrawal of the eucharistic chalice from the laity. This produced a situation in the Church's worship which was not only without Scriptural foundation but actually contradicted Scripture. More than this, it reversed a tradition issuing directly from the command of the Lord himself. When one compares this with the insistence that an all-male priesthood is an irreversible tradition in the eternal plan for the Church, the plain fact of a selectivity in tradition confronts us. Though the Scriptural evidence for this tradition is, to be generous, at the very best negligible, and though its real sources are readily traceable to the impact of a cultural and social gender-ideology on patristic exegesis and theologizing alike, it is still declared to be part of God's plan.

Again, the later growing opposition to the apostolical tradition of a married ministry (as recorded in Scripture), culminating in its final reversal with the imposition of clerical celibacy in the West by the twelfth century, is another example of the selective handling of tradition. Other traditions, stemming from apostolic times, underwent change and, as in the case of the ruling in respect of women worshipping with the head covered (1 Cor. 11:2–16), ceased to be regarded as applicable to the present. The question is, on what grounds is this selectivity based? Similarly, the *agapē*, testified to in 1 Corinthians, Jude, 2 Peter and elsewhere in Scripture, and continuing from the apostolic period until the third and fourth centuries in West and East, was gradually discontinued and often for valid reasons. Ambrose in Milan and Augustine in Hippo ordered that it should no longer take place and the Council of Trullo (692) ruled: 'The Agapae in churches are forbidden.' Here is the case of a genuinely apostolic tradition amply witnessed to in Scripture ceasing to have its original relevance for the life of the Church because of change in the Church's situation and environmental context. It is simply the process of revision which so often comes about when an inherited idea or practice is brought into life-relation with a particular 'present' and found to have no longer its original force and *raison d'être*. There come to mind Allchin's remarks on continuity and change: 'Do we remain true to the past by refusing to change, or by being willing to change?' Is it not a basically false assumption to make tradition and change antithetical, regarding tradition as static rather than dynamic, as fossilized rather than active? It is the fly-in-amber syndrome which occurs when *traditionalism is substituted for tradition*. As I have put it elsewhere: 'The former means the dead hand, the latter means a lifeline. The one is a stance of adherence, the other is a living process of transmission.'[37]

Nor is this assessment of what is a core-problem in this whole area confined to Anglicanism. Writing from the Orthodox perspective, Christos Yannaras makes precisely the same analysis of the modes of participation in ecclesial communion becoming autonomous and absolutized as values in themselves to be kept unaltered over time:

> In other words, traditionalism replaces the unique and vital functioning of the ecclesial tradition (the transmission of experience through types and forms of action which allow communion with life and existence) with multiple 'traditions' cut off from the transmission of communal experience. The 'traditions' are conceived as being autonomous 'religious' material, objectivized and unchangeable, transmitted from generation to generation as a precious ancestral legacy. The precious legacy must be kept unchanged, not because it concerns our life and the dynamic of our hopes, but because the safeguard itself provides us with good points of individual knowledge, gives us the title of faithful repositories.[38]

As one passes in review the thesis and the evidence for it which this book has attempted to set out in respect of the appeal to tradition and in respect of the question of the ordination of women, a judgment has to be made. 'If we must judge, then we must use our reason,' wrote Taylor, going to the heart of the matter in that way of his which often makes him as modern as he is Caroline. Otherwise, 'why do men dispute and urge arguments? Why do they cite councils and fathers? Why do they allege Scripture and tradition, and this on all sides, and to contrary purposes?' Reason, he insists, 'is instrument of all things else' but always right reason '*supposes the assistance of God's Spirit*'. It only comes into play 'when revelation, and philosophy, and public experience, and all other grounds of probability or demonstration have supplied us with matter, then reason does but make use of them'.[39]

It would seem to me that the evidence adduced in support of the claim for an exclusively male priesthood cannot be substantiated as conclusive and compelling either on the basis of the plain teaching of Scripture or on the basis of the apostolicity of continuing and universal tradition in the Church from the beginning. The hermeneutics of Scripture and of Tradition reveal the insubstantiality of that evidence. It is not that I dismiss lightly or factionally that position, having once held it myself, until, during the run-up to Lambeth 1968, prolonged reflection convinced me that there was no valid Biblical basis and no fundamental theological reason for denying the priesthood to women; that such ordinations were not against the divine order.

Our survey has revealed as a matter of record that Anglicans have never approached questions of doctrine or polity from the angles of fundamentalism or of traditionalism or of an infallible *magisterium*. Both explicitly and implicitly their criterion for authentication has been by means of the dialectical approach. It is the appeal to *all* the sources of authority, Scripture, tradition, reason and experience, taking account of their interaction and interrelation in determining what is genuine and permanent for the Church. Scripture is the primary source, tradition is the Church's developing apprehension of it and reason is the understanding of it by the individual and the community. *Over and through all three is the Spirit abiding in the Church, inspiring, guiding and enlightening.* Embedded in the process and in the functioning of this threefold appeal is the distinction between what is fundamental and what is secondary. This links in with the repeated Anglican claim to continuity in faith and order with the Primitive Church and with the appeal to it, which is always in respect of 'the prime doctrines' (Waterland) and not with regard to lesser or disputed questions (Jewel).

The distinction itself goes back to the Early Church in which the centrality of the rule of faith established that in importance of order there are primary and secondary doctrines. The rule of faith added nothing whatever to the Bible, and Hanson notes that it 'interprets and detects the drift or burden or main body of truth, the "scope", of

Scripture. This is as important a truth today as it was in the second and third centuries.' The fathers held that the rule 'was in its contents identical with the contents of the Bible' and could add nothing to it.[40] In fact, the formation of the Canon of Scripture had established that the Church saw a clear distinction between the revelation witnessed to in Scripture and interpretation, which is not to say that tradition as interpretation has not an important function: 'It means that there is a main body of truth, a "scope" to be found in the Bible, which the Holy Spirit intends us to find, and that the chief intellectual task of the Church is to find it, and find it anew every generation, and never to rest content with a final expression of it.' By feeding on the Gospel the Church produces tradition. The insistence that this tradition must be limited by the witness of the Bible is not 'to shackle a living faith to a dead document'. The Bible is not dead but *living*, faith-kindling and ever spiritually creative. Rather is it the *historicity* of the revelation, uniquely recorded in the Bible, which is the reason

> why tradition must be bound and restricted by this collection of historical evidence. To desire to emancipate tradition from this condition, to envisage for it some fairy cornucopia of developing doctrine which need owe no responsibility to historical evidence, is to evince an unconscious desire to abandon the Incarnation. Christian doctrine consists of the interaction of a living community and a body of historical evidence. This precisely reveals the nature of Christianity, its unique paradox of once-for-all event and transcendent Spirit.[41]

Hanson's analysis of tradition in the Early Church and his own exposition of the relation of Scripture, tradition and reason, are remarkably in tune with what we have uncovered of the Anglican ethos past and present. The wavelength is the same because there is, from Jewel to our own time, a recognizable ecclesial identity and one which claims continuity with the Early Church. Paul Avis speaks of *identity diffusion*, as when sixteenth-century Puritans kept looking over their shoulder at Geneva or when nineteenth-century

Anglo-Catholics 'aped Italian baroque spirituality'. He sees a contemporary case of this diffusion of identity when 'it is insisted that the Anglican Church cannot act – for example in ordaining women – until Rome and the Orthodox have given approval ... to thine own self be true!' Significantly for my whole theme he writes: 'The rebirth of identity comes about *through returning to our origins and applying the strength there derived to the problems of the present.*'[42] There, in a sentence, is the purpose and the project which this book endeavours to serve.

Notes

I The Spirit, Continuity and Change

1 R. P. C. Hanson, *The Continuity of Christian Doctrine* (1981), p. 72.
2 Olivier Clément, *The Roots of Christian Mysticism* (Eng. edn 1993), p. 9.
3 Nicholas Lossky, *Lancelot Andrewes, The Preacher (1555–1626)* (1991), pp. 338–40.
4 A. M. Allchin, *The Dynamic of Tradition* (1981), p. 2.
5 Richard Hooker, *The Ecclesiastical Polity* (1594, 1597 and posthumous), V, viii, 1–2.
6 Ibid., III, viii, 18.
7 S. Platten and G. Pattison, *Spirit and Tradition: An Essay on Change* (1996), p. 42.
8 Ibid., pp. 10–19.
9 Ibid., p. 59.
10 Ibid., p. 62.
11 Ibid., pp. 62–9.
12 Platten and Pattison would, I think, differ somewhat from me here; but compare R. P. C. Hanson, *Tradition in the Early Church* (1962), pp. 255–6.

II On the Limits of the Appeal to Tradition

1 Hans Küng, *The Church* (1967), p. 414.
2 Ibid., pp. 239–40; this is discussed by David L. Edwards, *What is Catholicism* (1994), p. 32: 'as this catechism demonstrates, "tradition" has developed in such a way that the *magisterium* demands the assent of reason and conscience by everyone, everywhere'; and cf. p. 38.
3 *Dogmatic Constitution on Divine Revelation*, 10 (*The Documents of Vatican II*, ed. Walter M. Abbott, 1967, pp. 117–8).
4 Ibid., 8.
5 Ibid., 10.
6 Ibid., 9.
7 Ibid., 10.
8 J. O. Johnston, *Life of H. P. Liddon* (1904), p. 134.
9 See E. J. Bicknell, *A Theological Introduction to the Thirty-nine Articles* (1936 edn), pp. 170–1.
10 H. R. McAdoo, *Anglican Heritage: Theology and Spirituality* (1991), pp. 5–8.
11 R. P. C. Hanson, *The Continuity of Christian Doctrine* (1981), p. 29.
12 R. P. C. Hanson, *Tradition in the Early Church* (1962), pp. 65, 74, 125; and cf. Bicknell, *A Theological Introduction*, p. 170: 'This view of the sufficiency of Scripture is for questions of doctrine the unanimous view of the early Fathers', and examples follow.

13 William Payne, *The Sixth Note of the Church Examined, viz. Agreement in Doctrine with the Primitive Church* (1687), p. 113.
14 William Laud, *A Relation of the Conference* (3rd edn, 1673), dedicatory preface.
15 Laud, *Conference* (3rd edn, 1673), p. 48.
16 Ibid., p. 49.
17 Ibid., preface.
18 Ibid., p. 63.
19 Ibid., p. 28.
20 Ibid., p. 34.
21 Preface to the *Conference* (1673 edn.).
22 Ibid. For a fuller analysis of Laud's views, see H. R. McAdoo, *The Spirit of Anglicanism* (1965), ch. IX.
23 McAdoo, *Anglican Heritage*, p. 8.
24 Quoted in P. E. More and F. L. Cross, *Anglicanism* (1935), p. 141.

III Anglican Formularies, Formulations and Tradition

 1 William Laud, *A Relation of the Conference* (ed. C. H. Simkinson, 1901), xiv, 385 and cp. 379)
 2 Francis White, *A Treatise of the Sabbath Day* (1635), pp. 97f.
 3 Lancelot Andrewes, *Opuscula* (posthumous, L.A.C.T. ed. Vol. 9, p. 91)
 4 *Interim Statement Towards Reconciliation* (1967), p. 7.
 5 Ibid., p. 8.
 6 William Payne, *Agreement in Doctrine with the Primitive Church* (1687), p. 114.
 7 Henry Hammond, *Paraenesis* (1656), ch. V, sect. 13.
 8 Hans Küng, *The Church* (1967), p. 16.
 9 Paul A. Welsby, *Lancelot Andrewes* (1958), p. 156.
10 Andrewes, *Opuscula*, p. 91.
11 Quoted in Welsby, *Lancelot Andrewes*, p. 156.
12 Welsby, *Lancelot Andrewes*, pp. 156–7.
13 Quoted in H. R. McAdoo, *The Spirit of Anglicanism* (1965), p. 330.
14 Lancelot Andrewes, *Responsio* (1610, L.A.C.T. ed. Vol. 8, p. 70).
15 Ibid., p. 25.
16 For an evaluation of Andrewes' theological position, see McAdoo, *The Spirit of Anglicanism*, pp. 320–36.
17 Quoted in W. Sykes, *From Sheldon to Secker*, p. 167.
18 Lambeth Conference 1948, *Report*, pp. 84–5.
19 Lambeth Conference 1968, *Report*, p. 82.
20 Ibid., p. 64.
21 Alan Robinson, *The Treasures of Jesus – a meditation on the Sermon on the Mount* (1994).
22 Lambeth Conference 1968, *Report*, p. 73.
23 Ibid., p. 63.
24 Nicholas Lossky, *Lancelot Andrewes, The Preacher (1555–1626)*, 1991, p. 340.

25 Lambeth Conference 1968, *Report*, p. 69.
26 A. M. Ramsey, *The Gospel and the Catholic Church* (1937), p. 64.
27 Michael Ramsey, *The Anglican Spirit*, ed. Dale Coleman (1991), p. 150.
28 Ibid., p. 34.
29 Lambeth Conference 1968, *Report*, pp. 82–3.
30 Jeremy Taylor, *A Discourse of the Liberty of Prophesying* (1647) sect. X(5).

IV Anglican Theology, Antiquity and the Fathers

1 John Jewel, *An Apologie* (1564) (see John E. Booty p. 130 for original pagination).
2 John E. Booty, *John Jewel as Apologist of the Church of England* (1963), p. 132, a book which must rank as the best modern study of Jewel.
3 John Jewel, *True Copies of the letters* (1560) (see John E. Booty p. 133 for original pagination).
4 John Jewel, *Defence* (1567), pp. 18f.
5 Ibid., p. 58.
6 George H. Tavard, *Holy Writ and Holy Church* (1959), p. 236.
7 Lancelot Andrewes, *Tortura* (1609), L.A.C.T. ed. Vol. 7, p. 96.
8 H. R. McAdoo, *The Spirit of Anglicanism* (1965), p. 5.
9 Richard Hooker, *The Ecclesiastical Polity*, V, viii, 2. For a further examination of Hooker's thought on these subjects, see H. R. McAdoo, 'Richard Hooker', in *The English Tradition and the Genius of Anglicanism*, ed. Geoffrey Rowell (1992).
10 Hooker, *The Ecclesiastical Polity*, V, vii, 1.
11 Ibid., II, viii, 5.
12 Ibid., V, viii, 1–2.
13 Ibid., III, viii, 18.
14 Ibid., V, lxv, 2.
15 Ibid., VII, x, 8.
16 Ibid., III, x, 7.
17 Stephen Sykes, *Unashamed Anglicanism* (1995), pp. 81–95.
18 Hooker, *The Ecclesiastical Polity*, V, lxii, 1–3 and 22.
19 Ibid., I, xv, 2.
20 Ibid., III, x, 5.
21 Ibid., VII, x, 8.
22 Ibid., III, v, 1.
23 Lambeth Conference 1948, *Report*, p. 85
24 Sykes, *Unashamed Anglicanism*, p. 93.
25 Paul Avis, *Anglicanism and the Christian Church* (1989), p. 273.
26 All citations from Hooker, *The Ecclesiastical Polity*, III, viii, 13–15.
27 Avis, *Anglicanism and the Christian Church*, p. 279.
28 Jeremy Taylor, *Ductor Dubitantium* (1660), Rule III (19), Reginald Heber edn 1828 Vol. XI, p. 439.
29 Jeremy Taylor, *The Real Presence and Spiritual* (1654), sect. I, 13, Heber edn Vol. IX, p. 432.

30 Taylor, preface to *Ductor Dubitantium*, Heber edn Vol. XI, p. 356.
31 Jeremy Taylor, *A Discourse of the Liberty of Prophesying* (1647), sect. VIII (4), Heber edn Vol. VIII, p. 84.
32 Ibid., sect. V (8) and (11), Heber edn Vol. VIII, pp. 18, 24.
33 Ibid.
34 Ibid., sect. VIII (1), Heber edn Vol. VIII, p. 78.
35 B. H. G. Wormald, *Clarendon* (1951), p. 252. See his Part III, I pp. 240–282 on the Tew Circle and for the same group see H. R. McAdoo, *The Spirit of Anglicanism*, pp. 343–55.
36 William Chillingworth, *The Religion of Protestants* (1637), p. 461.
37 Edward Hyde, *Animadversions* (1673), pp. 174, 189.
38 *The Golden Remains of the Ever-memorable Mr John Hales* (1659), ed. John Pearson, p. 31.
39 McAdoo, *The Spirit of Anglicanism*, p. 352.
40 Jeremy Taylor, *Works*, Vol. VIII, p. 84.
41 In fact I would maintain that Taylor is resistant to classification.
42 Taylor, *Works*, Vol. VIII, pp. 97–8.
43 Ibid., Vol. VII, pp. xvi–xvii.
44 Cf. Hans Küng, *The Church* (1967), p. 418.
45 Taylor, *Works*, Vol. VII, p. xviii.
46 Jeremy Taylor, *Unum Necessarium* (1655), ch. VI, sect. V (77), *Works*, Vol. IX, p. 50.
47 Ibid., ch. VI, sect. I (36), *Works*, Vol. IX, p. 17.
48 Jeremy Taylor, *Deus Justificatus* (1656), *Works*, Vol. IX, p. 341. See chapter I, 'Taylor's Theology: Modernity in the Use of Antiquity' in my *Eucharistic Theology of Jeremy Taylor* (1988).
49 William Payne (1650–96), quoted in *Anglicanism*, ed. More and Cross (1935), p. 141.
50 This and the following quotations from Patrick will be found in McAdoo, *The Spirit of Anglicanism*, with a fuller analysis of his theology (pp. 189–97).
51 Kenneth Stevenson, 'The Mensa Mystica of Simon Patrick' in *Rule of Prayer, Rule of Faith: Essays in Honor of Aidan Kavanagh O.S.B.*, pp. 126–154 (Collegeville Liturgical Press, 1996).

V The Appeal to Antiquity and Tradition in the Eighteenth and Nineteenth Centuries

1 See Norman Sykes, *William Wake*, 2 vols (1957).
2 Ibid., I, pp. 258–9.
3 *The Conversations at Malines, 1921–1925* (1927), pp. 38, 40.
4 Sykes, *William Wake*, I, p. 253.
5 Ibid., I, p. 264.
6 Ibid., I, p. 262.
7 Ibid., I, p. 297.
8 Ibid., I, pp. 28–31.
9 Ibid., I, pp. 63–9.
10 H. P. Liddon, *Life of E. B. Pusey* (1893), Vol. I, p. 413.
11 Peter Nockles, *The Oxford Movement in Context* (1994), pp. 105–6.

12 Ibid., p. 114.
13 Ibid., p. 119.

VI Some Conclusions
1 Paul Avis, *Anglicanism and the Christian Church* (1989), p. 273.
2 William Laud, *A Relation of the Conference* (1673), preface and p. 63.
3 *Pastoral Letter from the Archbishops and Bishops of the Church of Ireland*, dated Dublin, 14 November 1950.
4 John Bramhall, from the preface to *Schism Guarded* (1658).
5 'By its various enlargements of the ancient Catholic Creed to contain the twelve new articles of Pope Pius IV's creed, the two new articles of Pope Pius IX in 1854 and 1870 ...' (*Pastoral Letter*); 'the novel and supernumary articles of the Trent creed or creed of Pope Pius IV, imposed upon the consciences of men as necessary to salvation' (Daniel Waterland, *Works* (1823 edn), Vol. V, p. 277).
6 Avis, *Anglicanism and the Christian Church*, pp. 150–2.
7 Waterland, *Works*, Vol. V, p. 271.
8 Ibid., Vol. V, p. 319; William Chillingworth, *The Religion of Protestants* (4th edn, 1674), p. 65.
9 George H. Tavard, *Holy Writ or Holy Church* (1959), p. viii.
10 Waterland, *Works*, Vol. V, p. 330.
11 Ibid., p. 322.
12 A. S. McGrade, 'Reason', in *The Study of Anglicanism*, ed. Stephen Sykes and John Booty (1988), pp. 106–7.
13 Henry Chadwick, 'Tradition, Fathers and Councils', in Sykes and Booty, *The Study of Anglicanism*, pp. 91–105.
14 Jeremy Taylor, *A Discourse of the Liberty of Prophesying* (1647), sect. X (5), *Works*, Vol. VIII, p. 97.
15 Ian Bunting, ed., *Celebrating the Anglican Way* (1996), pp. 47–8.
16 Ibid., p. 25.
17 Robert Boyle, *Works* (1772 edn), II, 260.

VII Scripture and Reason (I)
1 Richard Hooker, *Ecclesiastical Polity*, II, viii, 5–7.
2 Ibid., III, viii, 14.
3 Ibid., II, vii, 6.
4 Ibid., II, vii, 5.
5 Ibid., I, xv, 1.
6 Ibid., I, xiii, 3: 'they are with such absolute perfection framed, that in them there neither wanteth any thing the lack whereof might deprive us of life, nor any thing in such wise aboundeth, that as being superfluous, unfruitful, and altogether needless, we should think it no loss or danger at all if we did want it'.
7 Ibid., III, vi, 1.
8 Egil Grislis, 'The Hermeneutical Problem in Hooker', in *Studies in Richard Hooker*, ed. W. Speed Hill (1972), pp. 190–3.
9 John E. Booty, 'Hooker and Anglicanism', in Hill, ed., *Studies in Richard Hooker*, pp. 223–4.

10 Hooker, *Ecclesiastical Polity*, II, viii, 7.
11 Jeremy Taylor, *A Discourse of the Liberty of Prophesying* (1647), sect. X, 5, *Works*, Vol. VIII, p. 97.
12 Ibid., sect. IV, *Works*, Vol. VIII, pp. 1–10.
13 Ibid., sect. I, *Works*, Vol. VII, pp. 443–56.
14 Ibid., sect. X, *Works*, Vol. VIII, p. 97.
15 Ibid., sect. III, 3, *Works*, Vol. VII, p. 497.
16 Ibid., sect. VII, *Works*, Vol. VIII, pp. 52–78.
17 Ibid., sect. VII, *Works*, Vol. VIII, p. 78.
18 Ibid., sect. X, *Works*, Vol. VIII, pp. 95, 98.
19 The sermon *Via Intelligentiae*, preached in Trinity College, Dublin, is in *Works*, Vol. VI, pp. 373–408.
20 Hans Küng, *The Church Maintained in Truth* (1979), p. 65.

VIII Scripture and Reason (II)

1 Simon Patrick, *A Discourse about Tradition* (1683), *Works*, Vol. VI, p. 425.
2 *Whichcote's Aphorisms* (1930 edn), 921, 916, 460.
3 Nathanael Culverwell, *An Elegant and Learned Discourse of the Light of Nature* (1652), ch. XI, p. 87.
4 Ibid., ch. I, pp. 1–7, ch. XVI, pp. 128, 172.
5 Ibid., 'To the Reader'.
6 Ibid., ch. XV, pp. 160–1.
7 Quotations from Henry More, the Preface General to *A Collection of Several Philosophical Writings* (2nd edn, 1662).
8 Ibid., Preface and Bk VIII, ch. XII, 2, 9.
9 Ibid. (3rd edn, 1662), Preface, p. 9.
10 Ibid., sect. I, II, LIV.
11 Ibid., 'To the Reader', p. xiii.
12 P. E. More and F. L. Cross, eds, *Anglicanism* (1935), p. 641.
13 Henry More, *Explanation* (1660), 'To the Reader', p. xv.
14 Ibid., Bk II, ch. XII (17–19).
15 Ibid., 'To the Reader', p. ix.
16 Ibid., 'To the Reader', p. xxix.
17 Ibid., 'To the Reader', pp. xix–xx.
18 Ibid., Bk VIII, ch. V (3).
19 *The Golden Remains of the Ever Memorable Mr John Hales*, ed. John Pearson (3rd impression, 1688), p. 44.
20 Ibid., pp. 45–9.
21 Ibid., p. 3.
22 Ibid., p. 8.
23 Ibid., p. 20.
24 Ibid., p. 31.
25 Ibid., pp. 28, 31.
26 Ibid., p. 65.
27 Ibid., p. 66.
28 Ibid., p. 25.

29 Ibid., p. 27.
30 Ibid., p. 7.
31 A. R. Vidler, *Essays in Liberality* (1957), pp. 21–8.
32 James Carpenter, *Gore, A Study in Liberal Catholicism* (1960), pp. 56, 61; A. M. Ramsey, *From Gore to Temple* (1960), pp. viii, 73–76, 78–83.
33 H. R. McAdoo, *The Spirit of Anglicanism* (1965), pp. 154–5.
34 *Of Conscience* (1650), *Of Scandal* (1650), *Of Sinnes of Weakness and Wilfulness* (1645), *Of a late or a Deathbed Repentance* (1645), *The Power of the Keyes* (1647), *The Daily Practice of Piety* (1660).
35 J. W. Packer, *The Transformation of Anglicanism 1643–1660, with special reference to Henry Hammond* (1969), pp. 88–9.
36 R. L. Colie, *Light & Enlightenment: A Study of the Cambridge Platonists and the Dutch Arminians* (1957), p. 21.
37 Packer, *The Transformation of Anglicanism*, p. 89.
38 Ibid., p. 90.
39 Henry Hammond, *Works* (L.A.C.T.), Vol. I, p. 182.
40 Ibid., p. 287. For an overall picture of Hammond's theology, see McAdoo, *The Spirit of Anglicanism*, pp. 358–68.
41 Paul Avis, *Anglicanism and the Christian Church* (1989), pp. 273–4.
42 Edward Stillingfleet, *A Rational Account of the Grounds of Protestant Religion: Being a Vindication of the Lord Archbishop of Canterbury's Relation of a Conference etc. From the pretended Answer by T. C.* (2nd edn, 1681), p. 243.
43 Ibid., pp. 189–91.
44 Ibid., p. 41.
45 Ibid., p. 267.
46 Ibid., p. 129.
47 Ibid., pp. 109, 111.
48 Ibid., p. 255.
49 Ibid., pp. 249–51.
50 Ibid., pp. 136–8.
51 Ibid., pp. 595–7.
52 Edward Stillingfleet, *Origines Sacrae* (1701 edn), Bk II, ch. V, v.
53 John Tillotson, *Sermons* (7th edn, 1688), pp. 3, 9, 16.
54 Ibid., p. 201.
55 Ibid., p. 254; and cf. *Sermons on the Incarnation* (1693), Vol. XI, sermons IV, V, VI.
56 Tillotson, *Sermons*, Vol. II, p. 86.
57 Ibid., Vol. II, p. 150.
58 Ibid., Vol III, sermon III and *Sermons on the Incarnation*, sermon II.
59 Tillotson, *Sermons on the Incarnation* (2nd edn, 1698), Vol. I, p. 63.
60 Ibid., Vol XI, sermons IV, V and VI.
61 Ibid., Vol XII, sermon VI.
62 Thomas Tenison, *The Difference betwixt the Protestant and Socinian Methods* (1687), p. 26.
63 Ibid.

64 Ibid., p. 30.
65 Sir Thomas Browne, *Religio Medici* (1642/3), ed. L. C. Martin, 1964, pp. 3–6.
66 *The Truth Shall Make You Free* (The Lambeth Conference Report, 1988), p. 81.

IX A Summation and Lambeth 1988

1 *The Truth Shall Make You Free* (The Lambeth Conference Report, 1988), p. 103.
2 Ibid., p. 104.
3. Ibid., (77), p. 101.
4 Ibid., (78), p. 101.
5 Ibid., (79), (80), pp. 101–2.
6 Ibid., (80), p. 102.
7 Ibid., (84), p. 103.
8 Ibid., (81), p. 102.
9 Ibid., (83), p. 103.
10 Ibid., (84), p. 103.
11 A. S. McGrade in *The Study of Anglicanism*, ed. Stephen Sykes and John Booty (1988), p. 106.
12 *The Truth Shall Make You Free* (89–90), pp. 104–5.
13 Ibid., (138), (141), pp. 114, 116.
14 Hans Küng, *Christianity* (Eng. trans. 1995), p. 603.

X An Application: The Ordination of Women

1 Stephen Sykes, *Unashamed Anglicanism* (1995), pp. 188–9.
2 *Elucidation* (1979), (2); *Final Report* (1982), p. 41.
3 *Report* (1989), (28), on the Ordination of Women, made to the General Synod of the Church of Ireland.
4 *Statement* (1973), (13); *Final Report*, p. 36.
5 Pope John Paul II, *Apostolic Letter* (1994), (4).
6 Lavinia Byrne, *Women at the Altar* (1994), p. 38.
7 *Report of the Select Committee on the Ordination of Women to the Priesthood and to the Episcopate as presented to the General Synod on 17 May, 1989.* (See *General Synod 1989 Reports*.)
8 Byrne, *Women at the Altar*, p. 42.
9 The correspondence is attached to the *Commentary* (1976) issued by the SCDF.
10 Lambeth Conference 1968, *Report*, p. 106.
11 R. T. France, *Women in the Church's Ministry* (1995), p. 73.
12 Ibid., p. 23.
13 Karen Jo Torjesen, *When Women were Priests* (1993), p. 33.
14 Ruth B. Edwards, *The Case for Women's Ministry* (1989), pp. 58, 70.
15 Ibid., pp. 83–5; Edward P. Echlin, *The Story of Anglican Ministry* (1974), p. 154.
16 John A. T. Robinson, *Redating the New Testament* (1976), pp. 68–70, 77–83, 352.

17 G. D. Fee, *Gospel and Spirit* (1991), pp. 63–4.
18 R. T. France, *Women in the Church's Ministry*, pp. 60–1; D. M. Scholer in A. Mickelsen (ed.), *Women, Authority and the Bible* (1986), p. 199.
19 R. T. France, *Women in the Church's Ministry*, p. 61.
20 Jerome Murphy-O'Connor, *Paul, A Critical Life* (1996), pp. 289–90, 356–9.
21 Elisabeth Schüssler Fiorenza, *In Memory of Her* (1983), p. 177.
22 Torjesen, *When Women were Priests*, p. 82.
23 Ibid., p. 37.
24 Schüssler Fiorenza, *In Memory of Her*, p. 309.
25 Torjesen, *When Women were Priests*, pp. 43–6.
26 Edwards, *The Case for Women's Ministry*, p. 84.
27 John Jewel, *Defence* (1567), pp. 18f. and *Defence* (1571), p. 202.
28 Edwards, *The Case for Women's Ministry*, p. 93.
29 See W. Gilbert Wilson, *Why No Women Priests* (1988), ch. 3.
30 Torjesen, *When Women were Priests*, pp. 43–6.
31 Wilson, *Why No Women Priests*, p. 34.
32 Torjesen, *When Women were Priests*, p. 52; Byrne, *Women at the Altar*, pp. 49–50.
33 Byrne, *Women at the Altar*, pp. 50–1.
34 Torjesen, *When Women were Priests*, p. 2.
35 St Thomas Aquinas (1225–1274), *Summa Theologica*, Third Part, Supplement, Q. 39.
36 Stephen Sykes, *Unashamed Anglicanism* (1995), pp. 94–5.
37 H. R. McAdoo, 'Richard Hooker' in Geoffrey Rowell (ed.), *The English Religious Tradition and the Genius of Anglicanism* (1992), p. 113.
38 Christos Yannaras in *Fundamentalism as an Ecumenical Challenge*, ed. Hans Küng and Jürgen Moltmann (1996), p. 76.
39 Taylor, *Works*, Heber ed., Vol. 8, pp. 97–98.
40 R. P. C. Hanson, *Tradition in the Early Church* (1962), pp. 125–6, 253, 259.
41 Ibid., pp. 254–6.
42 Paul Avis, *Anglicanism and the Christian Church* (1989), pp. 13–14, 20; and see ch. I, *passim*.

Index of Names